MW01486783

FUTURE PROOFING BY DESIGN

Creating Better Services and Teams in the Public Sector Through Design Thinking

by **Nilufer Erdebil**
www.spring2innovation.com

ISBN 978-1-7387679-1-5 (Paperback)
ISBN 978-1-7387679-0-8 (E-book)

First Canadian edition, 2023
Version 1.01.01

Table of Contents

Dedicated to all of those who are reinventing the future.

Introduction to Design Thinking

Future-proofing is about reframing the future. Future-proofing means creating products, services, and policies that can be used in the future even when the environment, technology, or situation changes. To future-proof by design we need to incorporate different perspectives — especially the human perspective.

Design thinking is a methodology and a mindset that can help make your products or services future-proof. It considers the people involved in challenges to highlight new insights and opportunities to future-proof by design. These new insights are key to updating and modernizing services and teams in the public sector.

What is Design Thinking?

If you're new to design thinking, you've come to the right place! By the end of this book, you'll have a high-level understanding of design thinking, when to apply this approach, and the mindset needed to use design thinking to propel your work forward. You'll feel comfortable with the design thinking process and understand its methodology.

Design thinking has been used in the private sector for decades to increase innovation, creativity, and sales. Design thinking is now being adopted more in the public sector for solving challenges involving people, such as those in HR, service delivery, regulatory burden, procurement, and customer experience.

Let's first define what we're talking about. Design thinking is a:

- Mindset
- Framework and methodology (to apply critical thinking)
- Method of gathering of a variety of perspectives
- Determination of problem(s) to solve
- Method of creating better services
- More rigorous approach to program, policy, and regulation design

Design thinking is going to change your life! One of the key components of design thinking is incorporating empathy and a better understanding of the emotions of those involved in the challenge you're examining. Empathy brings a deeper understanding of the people you are creating better solutions for, builds rapport, engages them further, and helps obtain buy-in. Empathy also allows for greater connections to happen across teams and with employees.

Design thinking and incorporating empathy will help you develop the right solutions for your clients and users faster. It will help your teams get along better and provide a path to innovation. More specifically, it's about having a growth mindset and engaging in continuous learning about ourselves and our clients.

It's helpful for decision-taking because it provides clarity on issues, establishes solutions, and enables easier decision-making.

Reframing is an essential aspect of the design thinking process and necessary for future-proofing. It is a skill that enables you to see a variety of fresh solutions to daunting challenges.

Reframing is about keeping your ears and eyes open to doing things in a different way. It also helps shed light on new angles of any issue from different perspectives.

In this book you will be guided through the mindset and methodology of design thinking, along with examples of how the public sector uses design thinking. We will walk you through our approach and how it can benefit your organization and assist your team in reaching their goals. You'll see several examples throughout the book that illustrate design thinking being applied to an issue from the start to the end of the methodology's various phases. At the end of each chapter the tools discussed in the chapter will be applied to the example, so your team can see how each step builds upon the previous steps.

This book is designed to support the creation of future-proof solutions. Your team may currently use lessons learned from the past to plan, which is part of future-proofing. But by using design thinking, your team will be able to better future-proof and adapt through better understanding those involved in the challenges and using that insight to ensure solutions meet their true needs. Essentially, your team will adapt for the future as they develop solutions.

Applying Design Thinking

Pause for a moment and think about these questions: Do your current policies, processes, programs, regulations, products, or services work? Have traditional models and methodologies worked well? How do you know they are working well? Or do you feel like you're battling last year's war?

In organizations there's often a lag in developing and executing on an improvement, which means problems that aren't as relevant are fixed while other, more urgent and emerging challenges fall off the radar.

Design thinking gives us the power to address not only today's challenges for end users, but also provides insight into client behaviours, values, and expectations so teams know where to improve next to stay future-proof. Design thinking allows foreseeing opportunities coming down the pipe so end clients can be delighted by teams anticipating and meeting their needs before they even know they have a problem — or know what they need!

For example, when thinking about current policies around collecting feedback, collaboration, innovation, travel policies, external services for citizens — whatever it is — are they up to speed? Are they the most current? Do they make an impact? And how do we know this?

Design thinking is about helping your team understand end users' needs better to discover their real challenges. This is an opportunity to do things in a different way by keeping our ears and eyes open. Once you see things from a design thinking perspective, you can't go back. And that's a good thing!

Design thinking supports the public sector in de-risking the future. The public sector has financial stewardship of taxpayer dollars, is responsible for regulation and policy direction, and is always in the public eye. There is a greater need to be more effective with resources. Thinking about the end user at the start helps de-risk initiatives and increases their effectiveness, because challenges are assessed from many perspectives.

When creating effective, efficient services that meet or exceed expectations, the first step is to examine the service from the perspectives of different types of users.

Clients can be either outside the public service or within (internal to the public sector).

External clients are people outside your organization who will use your products or services.

Examples of end users/end clients external to the organization could be:

- Citizens
- Businesses
- Non-profits
- Other government departments
- Other levels of government (including municipal/local governments, and provincial or state governments)
- International governments
- Whoever else uses your processes, policies, products, or services

There can be a personal component to it if you're thinking about using design thinking for your team within your work environment, or to increase resilience within your organization.

So, when do we apply design thinking?

- If your team wants to evolve, update, or innovate
- If your team wants to address a political change
- If your team wants to make a policy change or new policy direction
- If your team has a new boss or deputy, or your department has merged with another
- If your team has changes in your work environment
- If your team needs to respond to unpredictable or unprecedented situations
- If there are new laws or regulations passed that require doing things differently
- If your team is creating a new service, program, or policy design (or even a refresh)
- If your team is undergoing organizational changes
- If the policy isn't having the impact your team wants it to have
- If your team wants to change the public's perception of things such as, for example, fitness, mental health, or clean energy

It could also be to address service delivery challenges. If your team gets too many calls to your support desk, design thinking can help reduce that number. Design thinking can be applied to anything that can be improved and that also involves people, including large issues that impact people and people's behavior.

Designing for Customers, Clients, and Citizens

"If you think it's expensive to do customer research, what do you think it costs not to understand our customers?"

Can you guess which organization this quote came from?

It's a motto about understanding and designing for customers/citizens from HM (His Majesty's) Revenue and Customs, the U.K. revenue agency. It's about making sure the organization delivers for its clients, and making sure it adheres to the policies and regulations the organization has created. It's not just at a high level, either, but a deeper level to get into the minds of clients and truly understand what is important to them.

Internal clients are those within an organization. Examples of internal client relationships include:

- IT and business (working together to deliver a technology solution or service)
- HR and staffing
- Within teams
- Amongst departments (We've had experiences where one department created a tool for another department without talking to them, which led to inevitable adoption challenges. Design thinking can help circumvent this)
- Agile procurement (When you want to understand the people who will use your services and products before you even procure those services and products. In agile procurement, design thinking helps you understand what really needs to be procured through a

fuller understanding of challenges, and a determination of whether it's the right solution for those whom it is intended)

- Your team

We will really get into end users and end clients in the sections on empathy, personas, and unarticulated needs mapping and journey mapping, where we discuss more in-depth how to understand and identify end clients.

Design thinking is also great for mitigating the risks of innovation, because:

- It provides a better understanding of the challenge(s) and people involved (which ensures we create the right solutions)
- It involves end users in co-creation (by making users part of problem-solving)
- It actively listens for insights and adapts based on insights
- It supports in discovering and investigating unarticulated needs
- It provides more options (not just one solution, but multiple solutions that fit best for our clients)
- Design thinking is iterative, and we get better with each iteration

Consider how your team might apply design thinking to current policies, processes, programs, regulations, products, or services — anything that needs to be improved that involves people. Feel free to pause, grab your notebook, and jot down some ideas around applying design thinking to a specific challenge or area.

Design Thinking Roadmap

Design thinking is solution-based thinking. It's about understanding and delivering on the needs of users, understanding issues, and developing what's possible.

To best take advantage of the benefits of design thinking, we have a roadmap — a guiding light, if you will. I'll share the design thinking roadmap we use at Spring2 Innovation and highlight a couple other models out there. By the end of this chapter, we will have reviewed several different models for applying design thinking, and how to apply them to drive change and obtain buy-in.

We'll also walk through the basic steps of the process to make sure you're comfortable.

For the public sector, common issues for using design thinking could include:

- Requirements to update and adapt to changes
- Opportunities to improve
- Problems identified internally or from external sources

For the private sector, common issues for using design thinking could include:

- Shifts in consumer behaviour or purchasing
- Decline in market share
- Unhappy or increasingly unsatisfied customers
- Opportunities to innovate

Here's an example of a common design thinking model. This model is iterative — meaning you may go through the steps more than once. We start with the empathize phase, and then move into defining the challenge, followed by ideation, prototyping, and testing.

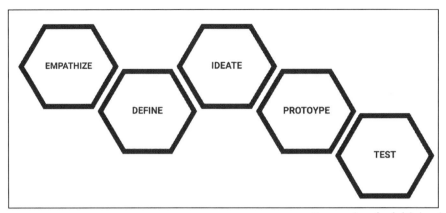

Source: Stanford d.School

Design thinking is a systematic approach that forces us to think about the full picture and helps circumvent our natural tendencies to jump into solution mode. We're often really good at diving straight into solution mode — which is actually the ideation phase of design thinking. It takes more conscious energy to pull back and think about improvements we're trying to implement, and even more effort to consciously pull back and think about who is involved in the challenges.

Let's look at two other common design thinking models. We won't use these as our roadmap for innovation, but they can be helpful for understanding the design thinking process.

This first one is the Double Diamond model. It showcases the divergence and convergence of thought that happens in design thinking. The process of discovery leads to divergence in thought, and then convergence as teams come together to define the problem. Teams diverge again as they ideate on solutions, and then converge once again to deliver those solutions.

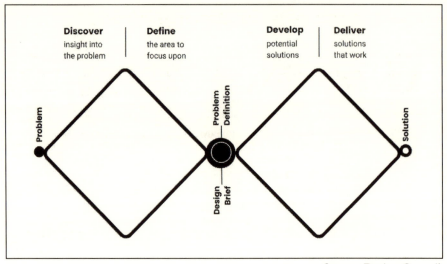

Source: Design Council

The second one is a 'what-if' model. This is a simpler model and can leave a lot to interpretation.

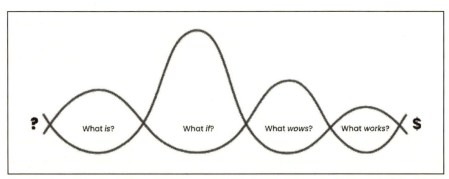

Source: Solving Problems with Design Thinking — Jeanne Liedtka, 2013.

The next diagram is the roadmap Spring2 Innovation has developed and uses based on our experience working with public sector organizations, especially government. We use this roadmap because the path of action is clearer and provides a more concrete structure and steps. This roadmap has seven stages where the first two stages are a precursor to the five phases of design thinking.

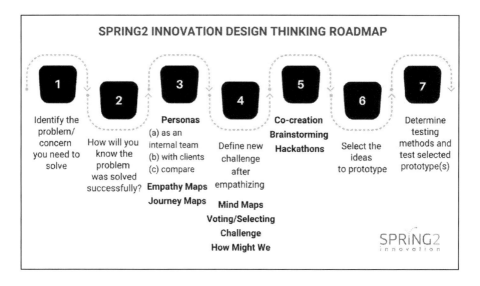

First, we begin with an initial problem or concern. Usually, within organizations, we know what we want to solve — or THINK we know what we want to solve — so we start with an initial problem statement and then come up with our measures of success. We ask ourselves, "What would success look like?" and make sure everybody on the team is aligned with the measures of success before we move on to discovering and learning about our clients. Once we understand more about clients in the empathize phase, we move on to defining the challenge, coming up with ideas, prototyping, and testing.

Communication throughout all the steps is important for both stakeholders and end users, especially if they're new to design thinking. It takes a different type of mindset to use design thinking — the more communication, the better!

We use this model for all our initiatives, including extremely complex challenges. After an iteration, your team will be able to walk out with a solution, no matter how simple or complex the challenge. Keep in mind that design thinking is iterative, so your team can go back to any step of the design thinking process. The more iterations you do, the better the solutions usually become.

Design thinking is great for driving change from the bottom up. Anything that involves people can usually benefit from design thinking.

Design thinking is also good for generating buy-in. People who will use your solution are the ones that:

- You need to understand better
- Will test your prototypes and provide insights
- Ideally co-create solutions with you along the way

If possible, try to involve champions of design thinking within your organization during the process, as they can help obtain buy-in from upper management.

Design thinking can also help rule out certain initiatives. If people aren't prepared to undergo the rigour around the design thinking process, it's an indicator that the initiative isn't ready to proceed. But without knowing your end clients' perspectives or providing options, the solution won't be as well-thought out as it could be. We've seen clients use design thinking as a measuring stick to determine whether people in their organization have thought through the issue and solution well enough.

Have faith in the process. It is an experience. Your team needs to go through it and feel the range of emotions for themselves and their clients, and see the insights and impacts from the process.

Identifying Problems and Measures of Success

Following our roadmap, let's now cover the first two stops on our design thinking journey — identifying problems or concerns, and measuring success.

In the upcoming sections we'll go through the five stages of design thinking. But before we do, we need to create the foundation for our work ahead.

The first two stages build this foundation by defining the initial problem or concern and developing measures of success within your team to determine what success looks like. Even if we don't know what the end service or process looks like, we need to talk about what we consider to be successful outcomes. Some might call it setting the table to ensure we're creating an environment conducive to success.

In the first stage we'll identify the problem or concern we want to solve. Sounds simple, and oftentimes we think we know the concern — so let's put that down. This will likely shift or get reframed as we progress through the design thinking process. For now, write down what you and the team think the problem your team is trying to solve. It will help identify the end users who will initially be involved.

Remember that design thinking is an iterative process, so even if you don't get the initial problem or end users right the first time, the nature of the process will make sure you go back and re-iterate the stages until you get it right.

Ensure that everyone understands the meaning of the problem statement, even for the initial problem. For example: What does increased impact mean to the team responsible for this initiative? If possible, state it in the initial problem statement.

We'll discuss more about how to state the problem in the define phase of the design thinking process, which involves defining the problem based on client insights. For many initiatives, however, this can take years to implement. It might be worthwhile to develop a high-level problem statement and then break it down into more manageable pieces. For example, there could be an overarching problem you want to solve in five years, but there may be a part of that challenge you can solve in the next six months to a year.

Challenges can be related to training, processes, systems, or people, and you want to make sure — if you can — to break down the problem into small pieces that are easier to digest, develop, and solve.

nking out challenges into segments, pieces, or phases helps ensure your team is keeping an eye on the bigger initiative while keeping the shorter-term work on track.

Measures of success, on the other hand, are what needs to be there for the team and end clients to feel like the initiative was a success at the end of implementation.

If the team doesn't have the same understanding of what success looks like, then even if the project is on-time and on-budget there will still be people who think it was unsuccessful. Not being aligned at the start can create these kinds of issues.

To avoid this, we recommend everyone on the team to think about their definition of success. Pull everyone together and ask the team to select their top three. This provides room for great conversation, debate, and intersection. This is an opportunity to get alignment from the start.

When identifying measures of success, also consider your team's timelines — is your team looking for something that will be completed in six months, two years, or five years? The measure for each will be quite different.

To this end, consider asking people: What measures of success are used in your work? Measures of success can include speed, convenience, price, cost, or user satisfaction. Being specific on how much of an increase in speed or what timeliness means adds more clarity to the measures of success and what the team is trying to achieve. Be as specific as possible.

Here's an example of a public sector organization that took the time to create measures of success with a client satisfaction feedback initiative. This organization provides services to other government departments. The services are assessed monthly through survey results. This organization selected five measures of success, which helped the team understand what needed to be delivered and what was important for the team to achieve.

1. Timeliness: Are clients satisfied with the amount of time it took to receive services? Are unplanned outages addressed and resolved in a timely manner?

2. Ease of access: Is service information readily available online or from my account team?

3. Positive outcome: Were customers satisfied with the services they received?

4. Process aspects: When customers have a problem or service delivery issue, does the organization keep them and their department up to date on the resolution?

5. Engagement experience: Does the account team manage the relationship effectively?

We often recommend being even more granular on these measures, like stating how much of an increase we're looking to achieve. If your team wants to increase something by 5%, for example, the challenge and solutions are likely much different than if your team wants to increase something by 50 percent.

We've worked with many organizations where measures of success had a huge impact on the alignment of the team. A few years ago, we worked with a small team of three people in the public sector. Before they started their project, we asked everyone to jot down their top three measures of success. After compiling a list, we realized there were eight measures of success among three people. That's not ideal. When so many things are considered a measure of success, everything diminishes in importance.

That's why we next had the team discuss and agree on their top three shared measures of success. This supported the team in attaining alignment from the start.

The measures can change as more information is learned about end clients, but it's very helpful to get the team aligned at the start through shared measures of success. Keep returning to the measures of success throughout the process — your team will have an opportunity to re-evaluate them later as they learn more about their end clients' measures of success. Keep your measures of success top of mind as your team develops prototypes and tests to ensure they meet these goals. A positive outcome is more likely to be achieved when measures of success are also considered, rather than just outputs.

Step 1: Empathize

Introduction to Empathizing with Users

Because the initial problem and measures of success are already identified within the design thinking process, we are now ready to begin the empathize phase.

Empathy is critical to succeeding in both our personal and professional lives. I'm going to walk through the different types of empathy and show why it's critical for the success of any project, procedure, or policy. We'll look at how to apply and enhance empathy internally within departments or organizations and externally with citizens, other departments, and industries. This chapter will also introduce the tools used for the empathizing phase of design thinking. We will discuss empathetic leadership and how to use empathy as a leadership skill.

By the end of this chapter, we'll be ready to dive deeper into personas, journey mapping, and mapping unarticulated needs.

Design thinking is a mindset that involves seeing things from a different lens to gain clarity on the problem. Empathy is about listening, observing, and understanding another's feelings and emotions and acknowledging them.

That's why empathy plays a key role in understanding end users better. Empathy helps us understand what their real problem(s) are so we can develop strong solutions. Design thinking helps make sure we're solving the right problems for the right people.

What is empathy?

- The ability to understand another person's perspective and feelings
- Learning to connect with end clients by seeing the world through their perspective (almost like having a camera on the shoulder of our clients, so we can see what they see)
- The ability to communicate our understanding of the emotions and perspectives of others

Empathy is also important because of the people perspective to organizations. Organizations are made of people, and people have emotions. Emotions often determine the decisions people make and the better we understand these emotions, the better we understand how people make decisions.

We often act and make decisions based on emotions. For example, when I went to buy my car, logically I should have looked for the most fuel-efficient model. But my decision-making ended up being based more on my feelings around how it felt sitting in and driving the car.

When leaders tap into positive emotions or engagements for motivation, it often results in better outcomes.

Knowing what people think and feel, along with their goals, values, fears, and expectations, helps us understand them better (and ourselves better).

Empathy is the major differentiator of design thinking and is a skill that anyone can learn. Anyone can be empathetic. The more you practice, the more you can improve your empathy skills. Focus on the other person's emotions and what positively motivates them.

Use these tools to learn and inject empathy into organizations and initiatives.

The Three Types of Empathy

There are three different types of empathy. First we have cognitive empathy, which is the ability to understand another person's perspective. Then there is emotional empathy, which is the ability to feel what someone else feels. Finally, there is empathic concern, which is the ability to sense what another person needs from you.

We don't use emotional empathy and empathic concern as much in the design thinking process. Rather, we'll focus on cognitive empathy, as it supports the design thinking process by helping us understand the perspectives of others.

Cognitive empathy enables leaders to explain themselves in meaningful ways — a skill essential for getting the best performance from their direct reports. An inquisitive nature feeds cognitive empathy. It requires leaders to think about feelings rather than feel them directly. You are a better decision maker if you can look at feelings objectively. Cognitive empathy also helps us give and take feedback constructively.

Theodore Roosevelt once said, "No one cares how much you know until they know how much you care" — yet this concept is often forgotten in large organizations. Demonstrating empathy towards your clients before offering a solution will go a long way as you move through the design thinking process.

Remember that your end users can be:

- Internal to the organization
- Citizens or businesses (external to the organization)
- Other government departments (OGDs)
- Our end clients serving citizens or businesses

Sometimes end users are our client's clients — for example, if we create an IT solution for frontline service agents, then our clients are the service agents and their clients are citizens. We need to understand both groups as we go through the empathizing phase.

It's also important to empathize with employees. Everyone experiences things differently, and building a culture of empathy is important to ensure people understand things from one another's perspective. It helps for building a culture of employee obsession, where we're focused on our employees and making sure the organization provides the best environment possible for them to do their best work.

To enhance empathy in organizations we need safe environments, trust, and openness to share new ideas.

But how do we operationalize empathy within organizations?

Let's take agile procurement as an example. In agile procurement, rather than putting out RFPs (requests for proposals), challenges are created for industry to solve. We need to get to know the relevant end users before issuing such a challenge (to ensure all end users' needs are addressed). As evaluation criteria are developed for the selection of the solution, look at it from the end user's perspective to determine what they want and need before procuring anything.

Another one of our clients asked for guidance around designing a training program at the national and local levels. As we went through the design thinking process with the client, however, the client learned in the empathize phase that the organization needed a national, not a local, training program.

We've seen this many times over — by bringing people together to talk about their challenges, real understanding emerges. We can then create a meaningful solution that addresses these needs.

We've also seen the need for operationalizing empathy in initiatives involving changing physical workspaces. There is a lot of emotion involved around the spaces in which we work. Design thinking can help pinpoint differences in perspectives before working together to find solutions: By understanding each other's needs, we can create prototypes that work for everyone.

We use three helpful tools during the empathize phase:

- Personas
- Empathy maps/unarticulated needs mapping
- Journey maps

We'll go further in-depth on these tools in later modules, but for now, let's get familiar with these tools as they relate to empathizing.

Personas, empathy maps, and journey maps are invaluable tools that will often be referred to as we move through the design thinking roadmap. We encourage teams to share these artifacts among other teams and stakeholders in your organization so a shared understanding of those being designed for emerges — and to ensure clients and their needs are always at the forefront of the design process.

Data is also a key part of the empathize phase. We encourage teams to strengthen user research and leverage any data they have, to add more dimensions to the perspectives of users.

How well does your team know your end clients and your end clients' clients? Oftentimes, it's not as well as we think. Clients appreciate when the needs of their clients are considered. Having all clients involved makes people feel included, makes them feel heard, and increases interactions.

Empathy as a Leadership Skill

To be a great leader, empathy is a critical skill. In this section we'll explore what makes a good leader, share the benefits of empathetic leadership, and identify actions a leader can take to be more empathetic. By the end of this section, we will understand how to become a more empathetic leader and delve deeper into a leader's roles and responsibilities.

Brené Brown is a research professor at University of Houston and author of *Dare to Lead: Brave Words. Tough Conversations. Whole Hearts.* She defined a leader as "Anyone who takes responsibility for finding the potential in people and processes, and who has the courage to develop that potential."[1] A good leader also inspires unlimited thinking and always looks for options and new possibilities.

Before we continue, consider characteristics that make a good leader. Consider how people feel when they're around them. Do they feel encouraged, motivated, or inspired? It doesn't have to be an executive leader — it can be anyone, in all aspects of our lives, like a hockey coach or teammate.

Here are characteristics of a good leader we hear often: Strategic thinker, honesty, decision-making capacity, good communicator, multitasker, resilient, inspirational, engaging, passionate, credible, team player, relationship builder, integrity, adaptable, approachable, trustworthy, confident. All these characteristics involve empathy.

"Executives who can effectively focus on others are easy to recognize," says the authors of the book *Empathy,* part of HBR's Emotional Intelligence Series. "They are the ones who find common ground, whose opinions carry the most weight and with whom other people want to work. They emerge as natural leaders regardless of organizational or social rank."[2]

Personally, I've leaned on one of my favorite leaders as a guide and sounding board when I needed advice. I could count on him to be there and support my decisions every step of the way. He's good at providing insights and helping me see things I might not have otherwise seen — all in an extremely supportive way.

One day I received a curt email from him, and I thought he was upset. Since we had a good relationship, I responded with, "I'm not sure I understand what you mean." Turns out he had accidentally pocket-emailed me! If our relationship wasn't as good and he wasn't as supportive, I might not have asked what he meant. But the nature of our relationship and his empathy allowed me to feel open to ask for clarification.

Great leaders understand their teams and clients at a deeper level, not unlike the concept of servant leadership. Servant leaders serve others through listening to and acknowledging others. Servant leaders look for insights and act on these insights.

What are telltale signs of a team with a great leader?

Team members are usually happy, which also impacts their home lives. They tend to have deeper and more satisfying work relationships. This is because great leaders are inspirational. Their teams want to follow them — they connect with their leaders, and great leaders bring out their best work.

Emotions have an impact on our work and is a huge factor in the success of organizations. **Great leaders are trusted, and people feel connected to them and their vision.** If your employees feel a positive connection with you as a leader and your organization, they're likely going to be more satisfied with their work, more engaged, more likely to put in extra effort, and less likely to seek other opportunities outside your organization. All these also result in increased productivity.

Empathetic leadership is essential in times of change — which is all the time, whether that change involves technology, environment, initiatives, teams, leaders, re-organizations, promotions, or locations — and that's just at work!

As a leader, never forget that emotion, not logic, is often the driving force behind all human activity. Empathy and a better understanding of the emotions of those around us is vital to success. Empathy helps understand our people better, build rapport, engage them further, and helps obtain buy-in. Empathetic leadership allows for greater connection to happen across teams and with employees.

Empathetic leaders work to build connections, leading to increased trust. **Trust is one of the key elements in developing creative environments, which then leads to improved innovation.** Because we work with people, relating at a human level is important, especially in government where our goal is to make a difference in people's lives. We can create a culture of empathetic employees and leaders by designing that culture.

There is a mindset component to culture that incorporates:

- Learning from situations, and an acknowledgement that failure is just learning new insights and information
- Asking for insights and thoughts of teams and your clients, rather than trying to convince them

Procter and Gamble (P&G), a global company that produces personal and home care products, has a mechanism to provide and receive employee feedback — the company asks its people to say "I have a view worth hearing, but maybe I'm missing something" — and then invite responses[3]. Successful organizations must have a similar employee obsession mindset, which requires advanced empathy skills.

Additionally, the impersonality of work can foster a lack of engagement. People typically stay in organizations for fulfillment, not just money. Feeling like they are contributing to, and are part of, something bigger is a more powerful motivator for employees than money alone.

How to Foster Empathetic Leadership

How can we foster a non-judgmental environment that embraces the consideration of all perspectives, while communicating that we understand and respect the feelings of everyone on the team or in the organization?

Here are a few ways leaders can demonstrate empathy at work:

1. Listen to employees, partners, and clients to fully understand what's going on

2. Ask questions that clarify assumptions

3. Create work environments where people feel safe to express ideas and concerns

4. Build connections

5. Enhance trust (which happens from building connections)

6. Foster an end client-first perspective

It sounds simple, but being an empathetic leader requires focus and conscious effort.

Indeed, leaders might be killing their organization's culture of risk and innovation without even realizing it. As a leader, you transfer your emotions to employees. Consider what you're transferring — we have all been in boardrooms or team meetings when a leader gets frustrated and the whole room shuts down.

Responding with anger or frustration erodes loyalty.

With frustrated or furious responses, employees become less likely to take risks in the future, because they worry about the negative consequences of making mistakes. Harvard Business Review (HBR) *Empathy* tells us that these kinds of interactions "Kill the culture of experimentation and risk-taking that is critical to learning and innovation."[4]

Empathy also means occasionally checking in with yourself:

- Self-identify your state
- Ask yourself: How do you feel?
- Is how you feel coming across to others?
- How will your feelings impact your decisions?
- How will all this impact the decisions of others?

We often don't think of these things consciously. But if we start, it is surprising the impact it will create on interactions, decisions, and communications.

Another concept we need to discuss is collaborative leadership.

A lot of people think collaborative leadership is group thinking. It's not. Being a collaborative leader still means making decisions when decisions need to be made.

In design thinking, collaborative leadership means looking at things from as many perspectives as possible — especially from your clients and within your team — and making decisions based on that information. It means being open to and asking for feedback. As you might have guessed, collaborative leadership involves empathy skills.

I'll leave you with another quote from Dr. Brené Brown: "Empathy is a practice that grows over time."[5] Remember that practicing cognitive empathy is like working a muscle. With increased repetition, the stronger it gets!

Consider what a leader can do to be more empathetic and to encourage feedback. We've listed some examples below.

- Active listening — if someone tells you something, respond and ask questions to showcase your curiosity and understanding
- Try varying approaches — some people like to be approached one on one, but others prefer a team setting
- Approach employees in an environment that makes them feel open to sharing feedback
- Be curious — ask questions and be open to learning new things during all interactions

Understanding Who We're Serving — Personas

Do users (or future users) want your team's services or processes? Do they use them? How do you know? If your team doesn't understand who their users are and their values, challenges, and expectations, you have a golden opportunity to improve processes, policies, and products or services using client personas.

In this section, we'll learn how to develop end user personas to design human-centric services or processes from scratch. This will change how your team views their end users! By the end of this section, we will understand personas, how to create them, and the best ways of applying the information gained from this critical exercise.

Our design thinking process can tackle any persona or type of environment, whether it's a finance team, an IT team, or an HR team. It doesn't matter what type of work they do — our process will help them.

Think about whether your organization's current policies, processes, programs, regulations, products, or services work. Perhaps they work for some end users but not all of them. Personas can help illustrate this.

g personas is the first step in the empathize phase and is a way of enting end user groups based on behaviour, demographics, and values. The purpose of personas is to create reliable and realistic representations of key audience segments, so your team can refer to them during the design process and understand end user groups better.

At the core, design thinking is about understanding end users' needs better to discover their real problems. When we understand end users' needs better, we can then clearly understand what the real problem(s) are, make decisions based on that information, and develop strong solutions. End users or end clients can be internal to your organization, another government department, citizens, businesses, or non-profits. End users are those who will use your product or service first-hand.

Personas identify who will use your team's processes, services, policies, regulations, grants, or programs, and then group them together based on behaviour.

For each group of end users, we'll create fictitious characters. In our practice, once we've identified a group of end users, we select an image, a name, and assign demographic data to illustrate the character. Demographics could be age range, education, family status, ethnicity, salary range, job title, major responsibilities, job level, and their physical, social, and technological environment. We may not use all of them, but we will use some of them.

Next, we identify and list their goals, challenges, values, and fears in relation to the initial challenge or the process, policy, or service. Teams can also add a quote that sums up what matters most to the persona. This finishing touch makes personas even more relatable!

With government personas, especially, we recommend listing demographics such as classification (if they're in policy, finance, computer science, IT, etc.), their level, and their department or sector.

Remember — it's super important to develop personas with end users whenever possible. Your end users can validate your team's personas and provide further insights that may have been overlooked! If a team created personas on their own and then created another batch with end clients, comparing the versions can help identify gaps in understanding of end users. Also remember that when talking to end users, make sure to begin with a clean slate.

If we want to get even more in-depth information from our personas, we'll also add their expectations and measures of success for the solution being created. Oftentimes expectations and measures of success can reveal valuable insights that can prove extremely useful before we move forward with solutions.

Here's an example of a public sector persona named Elizabeth, an executive in an IT organization. As you can see in the diagram, Elizabeth's key information illustrates what kind of environment in which she works and what she needs from a solution.

We see that Elizabeth is a part of a group that manages servers and databases. Some of her goals are to keep the infrastructure always running smoothly, and to help with troubleshooting.

Some of her challenges include the need to analyze and validate information and get to the causes of issues. She values correct information and not having to handle false alarms. She fears not being able to locate issues for her team and spending too much time fixing breaks. She expects that her tickets contain the right information so she can correct problems, and her measure of success is fixing those problems quickly.

Partner Persona:
Executive - Elizabeth

Demographics:
- Team manages servers and databases
- Ability to manage the business
- Trend analysis and dashboard presentation
- Requires fewer details

Goals:
- Monitoring solution that provides status of applications monitored
- Timely information on availability to speed up responses to incidents
- Reoccurring problems identified

Values:
- Using the system efficiently
- Getting cost efficiency (are we spending money wisely)
- User efficiency to enable support of more and more complex client applications/scenarios

Challenges:
- Unknown risks (don't know what they don't know) Are we seeing everything?
- Having a usable Graphical User Interface (GUI). User friendly to train employees effectively and have them easily navigate the system
- Large number of tools required to monitor and support current environment

Fears:
- Failure of service (especially not knowing why)
- Changes due to external systems that will impact my system
- Unannounced changes

Expectations:
- Quick notification
- Highly Available solution with clear and well defined Service Level Agreements (SLA's)

Measures of Success:
- Quicker response to incidents
- Overall improved health (measured by number of applications up)
- Positive feedback from clients
- Ease of training
- Intuitive Interface

As we think about end users, we need to consider if they might have end users of their own. For example, let's say we're creating an application for a client support agent. We want to be able to understand all the different types of clients support agents, AND the type of end users their job is to help or support.

In our work, as we create personas, we try to also create a visual. We find that even simple, hand-drawn persona visuals work great — if your team can't create one from scratch, they can always use images of superheroes, Lego, the Muppets, or Star Wars!

Investing time into high-quality personas can save time and money down the road by giving a vision of who the clients are and allowing your team to design solutions that truly address their goals, challenges and needs.

For example, in procurement, it's invaluable to understand everyone involved who will use the tool, and all the technology being procured — before the technology is actually bought — so the team can see things from all possible perspectives.

User personas can be both internal — such as IT and business groups within our own teams and departments — or external, such as businesses, non-profits, industry, or other government departments. They could also be citizens if we're creating policies, programs, or services. Personas can be of anyone who will be impacted by your solution.

One previous project, in particular, comes to mind when talking about personas. We began with an initial problem: We thought the team required a tool to streamline and standardize their tests. At the beginning, we had originally believed there was only one relevant persona — Marc, a fictious character who represented all users who would operate the testing tool to be procured. Marc was drawn on a flipchart where we listed all the characteristics (goals, challenges, values, and fears) of his persona.

PERSONA:
MARC

Demographics:
Age: 28
Male
Salary: $86,000
Location: Ottawa
Education: Business Degree
Marital Status: In a relationship (complicated)

Role:
- Maintaining systems/portal
- Helping clients troubleshoot issues

GOALS & CHALLENGES
- Fast, accurate testing/results
- Implementing new functions to better serve clients

VALUES & FEARS
- Functionality do not work
- Clients are not happy with changes
- Creating more work/issues with the current process

As we went through the process, however we asked ourselves if there were any other possible users — and we ended up creating two personas. Through our discussions we discovered that finance officers would also use the tool, so we created a second persona: Linda the finance officer.

PERSONA:

FINANCE OFFICER – LINDA

Demographics:
Age 40
Female
Salary: $80,000
Education: Undergrad and/or CPA
Family: Married with cats (3)

GOALS	CHALLENGES
• Efficient use of tool to test changes • Confidence in accuracy and fidelity of financial data	• The payment system is difficult to understand • Unfamiliar with system testing

VALUES	FEARS
• Accurate data • Timely payments	• Making mistakes when using the system • Not catching issues that lead to erroneous payments

SPRiNG2
i n n o v a t i o n

As we continued through the empathize phase of the design thinking process, we created empathy maps and journey maps to gather even more insights to inform our problem statement.

Along the way, we found that by going through each design thinking phase, we gained much more clarity on measures of success, priorities, personas, and the outcome that the team really wanted.

How Many Personas do you Need?

We're often asked during our training sessions: "How many personas should I have?"

Ideally you should aim for three to eight, but it really depends on the number of people affected by your product or service.

Multiple iterations of design thinking sessions will reveal more clarity around the number of personas you need. We've had sessions where we've started out with eight personas, but then found that four of them really didn't apply, while four new ones did. After going through multiple iterations of design thinking, we changed the personas significantly.

Keep in mind that you can use design thinking and personas for almost any challenge, and that the key to creating accurate personas is to create them with your end users.

Another great example of persona work is when we held sessions to design a travel program. We created personas and moved all the way through to the prototyping phase, doing sessions in-person, starting in the nation's capital. The team worked their way across the country to better understand the future users of the travel tool being developed. We began with eight different personas, but after the cross-country work the team was able to reduce that number to just four.

Let's look at another example of internal end users — employees. Employee experience is such an important challenge, and we've done quite a bit of work on it, especially around the perspectives of employees during an organization's transition to working from home.

During one client engagement, as more people started working from home, we looked at the challenges and needs of all types of employees in the organization. We looked at four user groups of those working from home — power users, leaders, trainers and facilitators, and office workers — and created a persona for each group with those end users.

The next illustration is an example of the office worker persona. We named this one Andrew, and he represents public sector managers working from home. We selected his demographics — he is between 30-40 years old, married, and lives in the suburbs with teenaged kids. He is tech-savvy, bilingual, and has a university degree.

PERSONA:
MANAGERS - ANDREW

ANDREW
Managers

Demographics:
- 30-40 years old
- Home with teenage kids
- Married
- Live in suburbs
- Tech savvy
- University Degree
- Bilingual
- Newly working from home

GOALS & CHALLENGES
- Not set up to work from home/no home office
- Not used to leading virtual meetings, unsure how to get engagement online
- Make sure his team understands their results
- Ensure good communication
- Technology challenges
- Limited network access
- Distraction
- Ensuring team unity
- Managing remotely, no direct observation

VALUES & FEARS
- Value convenience (no commute, save time & money)
- Fear that others don't think/know you're working
- Value fewer distractions
- Fear for mental wellness of the team

We then listed his goals, challenges, values, and fears around working from home for the first time. During these sessions developing personas with our end users — the employees — they felt they were being listened to, and that they had an opportunity to share their experiences. We were then able to use the information from those personas to better articulate the challenges of employees working from home.

~athy Maps

Empathizing with users and potential users is critical when developing a service, program, process, or policy. Building on the persona section, we're going to explore how to create an empathy, or unarticulated needs, map.

By the end of this section, we'll be able to use personas and empathy maps together to gather intelligence on users that will help improve existing products or services, revamp messaging, or launch a new policy, regulation, or service.

The creation of empathy maps is the second part of the empathize phase. Empathy maps are a great tool in the design thinker's toolkit and should be used whenever possible. They provide much more insight into the people and the problems at play.

During this phase you'll need to have identified and developed personas upon which you can base your empathy maps. Remember that personas are fictitious characters representing user groups we want to better understand. As with personas, aim to co-create empathy maps with actual end users.

Design thinking at its core is about understanding end users to discover their real problems. Empathy maps (or unarticulated needs maps) allow a deeper understanding of end users' needs, thoughts, and feelings. By understanding end users, we can understand their problems better and develop strong solutions.

We often THINK we know the problem that needs to be solved. But through understanding users at a deeper level, we can better understand all issues at play and begin to break them down into more manageable pieces. This is extremely useful in the public service, as many of its problems are complex and have a huge impact among organizations and citizens. Sometimes it's a technology problem, other times a policy problem.

Either way, by digging deeper through personas and empathy maps, design thinking can reveal other unexpected challenges around people, processes, technology, training, or other areas that must be addressed (either as part of the initiative or separately).

Like personas, end users can be internal or external to your organization, another government department, citizens, businesses, or non-profits. End users are those who will use your product or service.

Sometimes, in organizations that have a harder time accepting the term "empathy maps", we refer to them as unarticulated needs maps. We've found that different wording can strike a different chord and resonate better with some people. You can select either term depending on the audience. At their core, empathy maps and unarticulated needs maps are about understanding the thoughts and emotions of end users and getting a glimpse of what's going on in their minds.

Empathy maps should be based on an existing persona. We want to explore what our persona says, does, thinks, and feels about the problem — whether it's operating a tool or software, visiting a client care center, onboarding employees, or completing an online form.

Often what people say and do are two different things, but either way, saying and doing can both be observed and measured. Thinking and feeling, however, are both unarticulated and, therefore, harder to observe and measure.

It's fascinating when we look at the different people involved in challenges within organizations, they usually think and feel very similar things, but don't express them. We're so used to creating outputs without considering the people involved. That's why mapping unarticulated needs really allows us to get at what people truly think and feel, so we can address their true problems.

How to Create an Empathy Map

To create an empathy map, in each quadrant, brainstorm what your chosen persona will likely say, do, think, and feel as they use your product, service, or solution.

If your organization is new to empathy mapping, it may take a few iterations for everyone to understand the value of empathy maps. To normalize empathy mapping we find it helpful to provide examples of empathy maps that have either been created in organizations already, or to show examples from similar organizations.

Here's an empathy map we did for our persona, Marc, from the section on personas. When we did this session in-person we listed his goals, challenges, values, and fears on the flipchart paper for participants to refer to as we created his empathy map. In this case the challenge was around Marc's experience using a testing tool, and we captured what he said, did, thought, and felt as he used the tool.

SAY	THINK
• This is cumbersome and repetitive	• I wish someone else could be doing this
DO	**FEEL**
• Recording steps taken during testing and taking screenshots	• Happy with no issues • Bored/ tedious work

This is another example from past work we did using a persona of a public sector decision-maker. We did the session in-person, then input the data into an MS Word template (you can use whatever format or software makes it easier for you to analyze and assess the information).

EMPATHY MAP

Persona: Decision-Maker

SAY	THINK
• Assure clients/customers about service • Ask for better info to support decisions • Ask for consistent info from various parts of the organization	• Can I trust this report/info? • What info do I need to make decisions about our operations? • What are our customers thinking about our services?
DO	**FEEL**
• Reviews stand reports/dashboards on Ops, projects, initiatives, etc. • More decisions on day-to-day Ops and future actims, investments • Provide information to partner organizations, clients and policy shops.	• Worry about client satisfaction/perception • Worry about meeting performance objectives • Questions about future actims (worry) • Making gut decisions rather than based on evidence

In the further example below we see an empathy map of a public-sector employee who has been transferred to another department.

SAY	THINK
• What can I do to help? • What can I read/do I need to know? • What are my responsibilities? • How do I get my tools? • Can you review this?	• I'm so lost! • They are so disorganized! • Who's that? What's that? • How do I figure this out/who can I ask? • Is what I'm producing meeting expectations?
DO	**FEEL**
• Find contact/mentor to guide me • Gather documents/resources to start work hired to do • Introducing themselves throughout organization • Call IT helpdesk	• Anxious/stressed • Frustrated • Confused • Eager • Motivated • Self-doubt • Stupid!

It's easy to construct empathy maps both in person and in virtual environments when the right environment and safe space is set up to allow for sharing thoughts and emotions. We use different types of software to create digital empathy maps. Digital formats make it super easy to share across your organization, but we suggest using whatever you are most comfortable with. The idea is to get at the persona's articulated and unarticulated needs so we understand them better.

Ensure empathy maps are developed with end users and partners. Whether it's virtually or in-person, we recommend doing them in a group environment, either with one group of the same persona together or multiple groups of different personas on the same team.

For empathy maps or unarticulated needs maps to be effective, there needs to be faith in the process. This is especially important for organizations who have never worked with empathy maps before. We find that the most resistant organizations to using empathy maps often benefit from them the most. Adopting empathizing tools for solving challenges allows organizations to gather valuable information quickly to truly understand the people involved, enabling the organization to move towards the right solution faster.

To help get you started on empathy maps, we've provided an empathy map template that can be downloaded from this book's website at https://futureproofingbydesign.com. Remember to co-create empathy maps with representatives of your user persona groups where and whenever possible.

Journey Maps

Has your team undergone the end-to-end experience of its own service, program, or regulation? Are they aware of any sticky points across any channels that may impact the experience of your team's users or partners?

We've already learned about and created personas and mapped the articulated and unarticulated needs of users.

By the end of this section, we'll understand the importance of journey maps and how to develop them.

This is a continuation of the empathize phase, where we have already identified and developed personas upon which to base journey maps. Remember that personas are the fictitious characters we want to understand better. Empathy maps can also assist during the creation of journey maps.

Journey maps are visual representations of the user persona's end-to-end experience and often include both current and future maps. Journey maps include the steps the user takes, and lists the parts of the journey working well and other parts that aren't. The reason we list both is to ensure we don't change what's working.

Client/customer journey maps include how end users and partners interact with your process, policy, program, or service. In the public sector we can develop journey maps for clients or citizens. We want to make sure we create at least one journey map per persona, and one journey map for each channel the persona interacts with (such as online, through a call center, in retail, or in person).

Keep in mind that a channel is a path that users take and that, especially for organizations with many possible channels, this could end up meaning A LOT of journey maps. We once spoke with a telecommunications company that had 17 different channels. Journey maps can also be helpful for cross-channel user experiences.

Here's an example of a journey map for a customer going to a coffee shop. We want to understand a customer's orientation — a bottom-up perspective. Many of us can probably relate to this example as an end user of coffee shops. Because this channel is the in-person journey, we start the journey as the customer walks into the store.

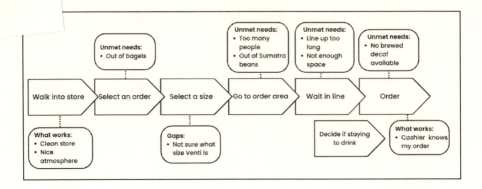

It's important to note that the journey could start even earlier: We could look at how the customer arrives at their location by looking at what happens outside the store. But the channel we've selected here is the in-person journey:

- A customer walks into the store. What works well is that it's a clean store and a nice atmosphere.
- They select an order while noticing the store is out of bagels, which is an unmet need.
- They then decide on a beverage size but aren't sure of the store's drink sizes, which is a gap in understanding.
- Next, they go to the appropriate area to order. Some of their unmet needs are that there are too many people in line, and that the store is out of Sumatra beans.
- They wait in line, where the lineup is too long and there isn't enough space (further unmet needs).
- They make their order. The cashier already knew their order, which was a huge bonus. However, another unmet need was that there was no brewed decaf available.

If you have them, process maps are a great place to start before creating journey maps, although your journey map could of course be different than the process map.

Involve end users throughout the creation of journey maps as well. It's fascinating to see what happens in organizations versus what's in the process map: Sometimes processes have changed and shifted, and the process maps don't always capture those changes. Additionally, people don't always follow the process map, so the end client may experience something completely different.

Think about when the user's journey starts and where it ends. In our coffee shop example it started when the customer walked into the store, and ended once they had their coffee. But we could change this and choose to end the journey map when the customer finishes drinking the coffee (whether they stay in the store or take it home).

This is important to think about because our concept of when things start and when they stop can be different. Say, for example, I'm the end user at my home. When I ask my kids to take out the garbage, they think it means packaging up the garbage and taking it to the garbage can outside. But as the end user, I also want a clean garbage bag replaced in the garbage can inside. For me, the end of the process is when the trash is taken outside and a new bag is in place.

The above illustrates why it's crucial to think about what finished looks like from your end user's point of view — what does the end look like for them? That will help your team determine the appropriate end point of the journey map.

Here's an example of a journey we did with a past client. We divided the journey map into three sections: Scoping, testing, and implementation. We then did mini-journey maps for each section.

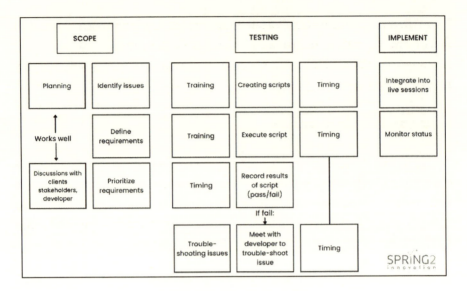

We could also include feelings and emotions in each step of the user journey. These are important because users might become happy, stressed, or upset at any step along the way.

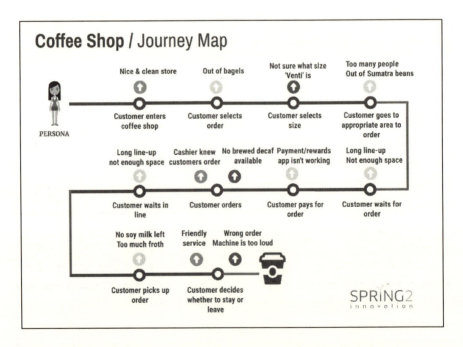

The example above is a journey map created using Venngage.

The arrows in the diagram indicate where in the journey the custom a positive, neutral, or negative experience. We demonstrate how journey maps fit into the overall design process. We also want to create a journey map for each channel your user persona may use as they interact with your team's process or service, using the information in their empathy maps and personas as a guide.

In the diagram below, we demonstrate how journey maps fit into the overall design process. We want to create a journey map for each channel your user persona may use as they interact with your team's process or service, using the information in their empathy maps and personas as a guide.

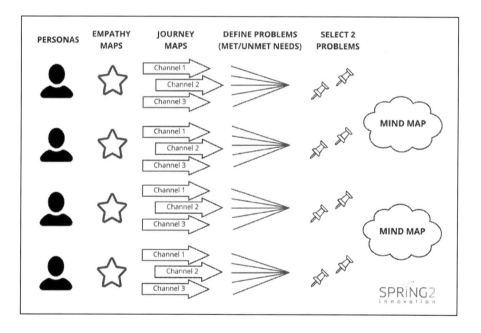

It takes time to develop great journey maps. Where and whenever possible, create journey maps with end users who are going through these steps in real life. Keep in mind that trends change over time, so what may work great today may not be optimal in two years.

Make sure to take time with journey mapping. If not, there is a risk of making assumptions about the user's journey.

Journey maps will help find additional challenges for personas and help define the primary challenge. Remember, try not to change things that are working well.

How do we select which channel to start with? Consider going with the most recurrent. To come back to the coffee shop example, most people physically walk into the store to buy coffee, so for this one, we started with the in-store channel.

Let's look at a public sector example. In this example, we're going through the process of obtaining a passport.

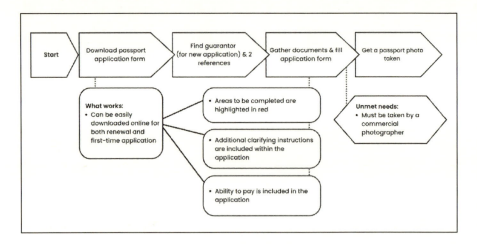

First, the user needs to download the passport application. It works well because those looking for either renewals or first-time applications can easily download it online. Next, they need to find a guarantor and two references. They must then gather the documentation and complete the application form.

What works well here is that the areas of the form that need to be completed are highlighted, additional clarifying instructions are included in the form, and the ability to pay is also included. The user must then get passport photos taken. The unmet need that doesn't work well for them is that the photo needs to be taken by a commercial photographer.

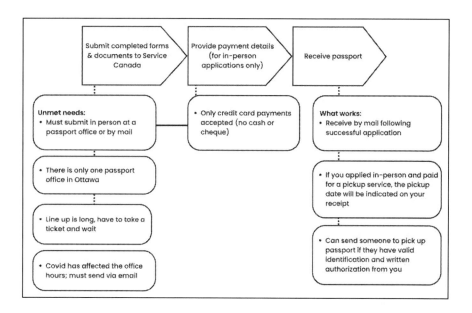

Next, they submit the completed forms to the passport office. What doesn't work well is that there's only one passport office in the city, the lineups are long, and they have to take a ticket and wait. The pandemic has also affected the office's availability and staffing. Once their ticket is called they must then provide their payment details. What doesn't work well here is that the office only accepts credit cards — no cash or cheque.

Finally, the passport is received by the applicant. What works well is that they have multiple options: They can receive it via mail, at a physical pick-up location, or they can authorize someone to pick up the passport on their behalf.

Let's look at another example journey map. This one is for someone looking to apply for government assistance after losing their job.

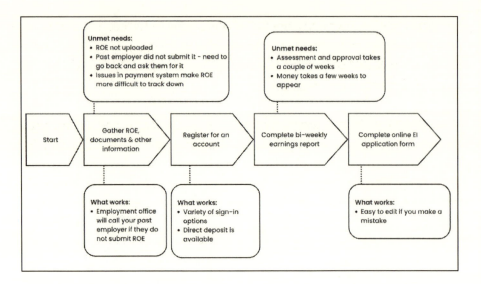

First, the applicant gathers and submits their record of employment (ROE) and other applicable documentation showcasing where they worked and for how long. What works well is that the employment office will call the applicant's past employer if the ROE isn't submitted. What doesn't work well is that the ROE was not uploaded, the past employer did not submit it, and issues in the pay system made the ROE difficult to track down.

The next step is to register an account online. The applicant can use their bank card or create a government account. Direct deposit is also available. The applicant next completes their earnings report, which determines the amount of assistance they will receive. What doesn't work well is that they must then wait a couple weeks for the assessment to be approved and completed, which means funds may take a few weeks to appear in their bank account. The last step is the completion of any remaining information in the application, which is easy to edit if you make a mistake.

Journey maps work well when you already have prior processes or services in place. If you don't, you can create a future or ideal journey map.

Alternatively, if other departments or organizations have a simil. understanding the journey/experience around their service may l. come up with better solutions — incorporating more of what work and solving existing challenges.

Future journey maps tend to be part of the ideation and prototyping phases in the design thinking process. When creating future journey maps, ask your team: "What would the ideal journey be like for our user persona?" What do they want the future to look like? This will provide insights into challenges and how your team's end users would like them solved.

As journey maps are created, think about possible future changes your team can foresee either in your sector, the economy, or your organization. This will help visualize what that journey will look like in two to five years.

End users already have increased expectations based on other products and services they use in other areas of their lives. Your team needs to identify these expectations and ask themselves how they can build them into the future (or ideal) journey map.

Design Thinking in Action: The Passport Application, Part 1

Here's a demonstration of how to practically apply the empathize phase to a public sector challenge — in this case, the passport application process.

The illustrations were generated using Miro, a virtual visual collaboration tool.

In this example, our persona, Stevie, is planning to travel abroad in eight weeks. But Stevie realizes that their passport is expiring in a month. Stevie plans to submit the passport application in person at the passport office.

Stevie's persona, empathy map, and journey map of renewing their passport are shown in the next few pages. The illustrations give us insight into Stevie's challenges and pain points.

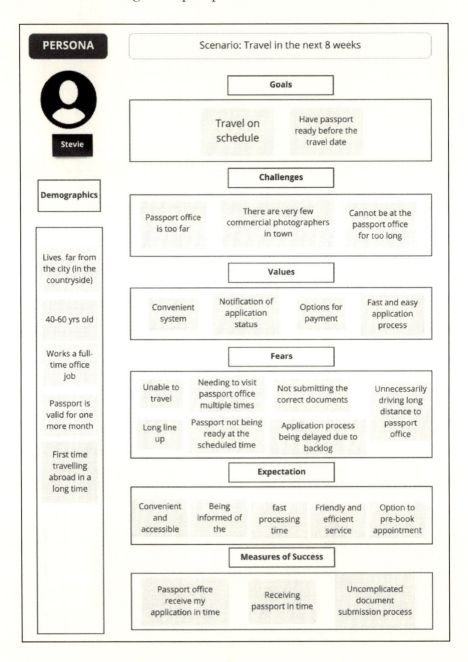

Step 1: Empathize

EMPATHY MAP

Stevie

SAY

I cannot wait to travel!

Where is my old passport?

What a long drive to passport office!

I hope this is quick...

DO

Gather all documents

Submit documents

Check website for updates

Wait for the passport completion

Take a passport photo

Go to passport office

THINK

Should I walk in or book an appointment?

Should I mail this or go in person?

Hmm...who will be my references?

The application form instructions are clear - this should be easy!

Will I be able to travel?

Will my passport be ready in time?

Will they notify me when the passport is ready?

FEEL

Nervous about all the hotel/bookings that they already paid

Concerned of the possibility of going back and forth to passport office

Anxious about taking time off the regular work schedule to go to passport office

Frustrated with inefficiency of the application process

Articulated

Unarticulated

57

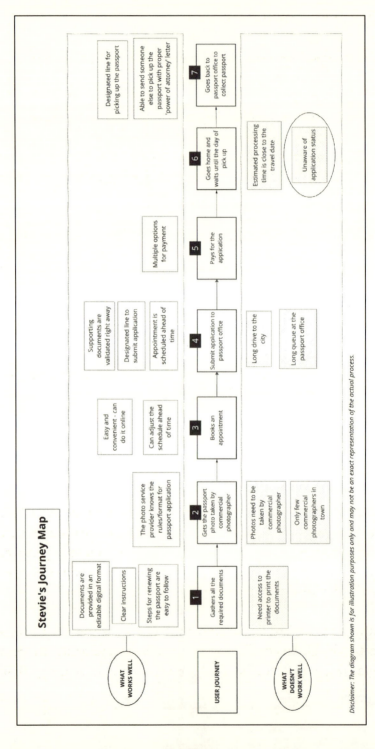

Stevie's Journey Map

Disclaimer: The diagram shown is for illustration purposes only and may not be an exact representation of the actual process.

Summary — Empathize Phase

In the first step of the design thinking process, we have discussed:

- What empathy is
  - Human interaction with an intent to understand

- Why empathizing is important in the design thinking process
  - To ensure we are addressing the right issues from the outset

- Who to empathize with
  - Identifying the end-users

- How to enhance empathy within organizations
  - Promoting a culture of understanding versus controlling

- Empathy as a leadership skill
  - Understanding the needs and desires of those we can influence and inspire

- Personas, empathy maps and journey maps
  - Tools to support the effective execution of design thinking

People are always at the heart of any project and using an empathy-driven approach will allow you to connect with the people involved. By actively listening to your end users and seeking to understand their perspectives, you will be more equipped to uncover their true needs and challenges and ultimately provide them with effective solutions.

Empathy is not limited to the empathize phase — it is a key element of the entire design thinking process! It will be important to continue practicing empathy as you proceed to the next phases of design thinking.

Step 2: Define

Defining Your Problems

We're now at the second phase of the design thinking process. The define phase is one of the most important phases because it affects how your team approaches the following phases, from ideation to test. In this chapter we'll discuss how to define your problem, how to frame it as a problem statement, how problem definition impacts decision-making, and how to break down a challenge that has multiple sub-problems.

As we define the problem we will dig deep to uncover and understand the real challenge(s). We will create a problem statement by providing clarity and conciseness to the problem for those involved in the design process.

We'll discuss reframing the problem and gaining new insights by challenging assumptions. We will also delve into the tools we use to further explore the root causes of the challenge, including the five whys, fishbone diagrams, and mind maps.

Many of us are good at coming up with solutions, but it takes discipline to pull back and look at the real problem. That's because there's a lot of work that must happen before we define the problem (or problems). It seems (and is!) a lot of upfront work, but it will make everything your team does later move much faster and be more effective and easier because we know with greater clarity what needs to be solved.

How can you be sure you're solving the right problem?

Design thinking helps in this regard because it's about looking at the challenge before coming up with its solution. A solution can only be as good as the definition of the problem it's trying to solve.

Stephen Hawking once said, "The greatest enemy of knowledge is not ignorance, it is the illusion of knowledge." By this he meant that we need to be aware of what we THINK we know, and to never take it as gospel — always confirm your knowledge or understanding. In design thinking we define our challenge with additional knowledge gained during the empathize phase, which has been validated by our end users.

Defining what it is we're trying to solve is about getting at the heart of the issue or issues. We want to build and design solutions that respond to end-users' actual needs and challenges.

Whether you're in IT or HR, operations, policy, finance, or other corporate functions, it's easy to understand the general problem space and build complicated solutions that don't address the underlying issues. But we want to focus on assessing business benefits rather than just executing projects within the scope, on time and on budget. That scope may not have been the right scope to solve the underlying issues to begin with.

Decision-making is about first understanding the challenge and then making the right decision. The clearer the challenge, the easier it is to improve the outcome.

Design thinking is about getting clarity on an issue so it's easier to make decisions and act. That's why it's important to spend as much time as needed in the define phase, because this is where we define the problem.

Start with the initial problem or concern, develop your measures of success, then empathize, reframe, and redefine the problem based on this information.

When it comes time for decision making, we're in a better position to come up with options and take action because we have a well-defined problem. It's a common refrain that if you only see one solution to an issue, you don't understand the issue. It's true. Understanding the challenge allows you to come up with far more solutions.

Having said that, the define phase is based on information that has been gathered so far. You may find a need to divide the challenge into multiple challenges, phases, or smaller projects to take the needs of individual groups (that have different needs and may use different business processes) into account. All this begins in the define phase.

One of our clients once told us, "Having a toolkit to actually force us and our clients to approach the problem, without presuming that we know what the answer looks like, is actually liberating and also seems to lead us to better outcomes."

Another one of our clients said, "There is no such thing as just an IT project. There are business projects and business problems to solve, and IT may be one of the levers that needs to be pulled to make that happen."

Because design thinking is about looking at issues from different perspectives at a deeper level to identify all the different parts, your team may also potentially identify different phases or parts of the challenge. There may be one or multiple challenges. Some of those issues may not be in your team's scope to be able to change or address, but they are part of your initiative's ability to succeed. They must be noted and assigned to others for oversight.

When framing the challenge, phrase it in a positive way to create a positive focus on solutions. For example, rather than saying a system or process is slow, reframe as: We want to increase the speed of the system/process. If we can identify how much we want to increase it by, even better. We can then say: We want to increase the speed of the system/process by 75 percent.

It's also important to be specific with wording. Ensure everyone has the same understanding of each word in the problem phrasing. If we say, "We want to increase the impact of our solution," ensure everyone is on the same page about what "impact" really means.

Using the statement "How might we...?" at the start of your problem definition will help put the statement in a positive, collaborative format that enhances the collaborative and solution-oriented mindset of your team, clients, and partners. How might we (HMW) is a common design thinking technique that is useful to as we define and reframe the problem and then bridges us towards ideating on possible solutions to solve our clients' problem.

Executing the Define Phase

First, list all the unmet needs identified from the empathize phase's personas, empathy maps, journey maps, and any other data you have.

Next up is synthesizing all this information. There are different ways of doing this. We recommend synthesizing data around each persona by identifying their key challenges. Bring these challenges together and look for commonalities before joining all the data. Remember that not all personas have equal value: Some may be more important based on your original challenge and measures of success (these may change as you discover more information). We often use this process to better understand challenges from different perspectives.

It also helps to synthesize information as a team, because it provides insight into all the challenges while everyone is together. Using this process helps teams set priorities.

There are different ways of analyzing information generated from the empathize phase. One way is to create a mind map from each persona that includes all their challenges. Remember that these challenges include information gleaned from the personas, empathy maps, journey maps, and other ethnographic research your team completed.

Another way of synthesizing information from the empathize phase is to bring all challenges from all personas together into one format. We like to use mind maps, so we suggest bringing everything into a single mind map where all challenges are all equally visible. We'll discuss mind maps in more detail later in this chapter.

There are also different ways of determining what challenge(s) need to be pursued. One method we often use is voting, either through one vote per person or weighted voting. Weighted voting involves giving certain groups or leaders more voting power — you can give them two or three votes while other groups get one. Initiatives with lower price tags or shorter timelines might also get a higher weighting. What's important is to pull back and consider how you will select the challenge you want to pursue.

We've often found that the most recurring challenges tend to percolate. It's important to pay attention to these recurring themes as we move along. There may be barriers that end users are not aware of (although we recommend sharing these as you define challenges together), or there could be external, political, or technological shifts in the organization. At the end of the day, your team still decides what the challenge should be. We can gather information and process it, but the team and leader decide the issue and, ultimately, what moves forward.

It can be valuable to pull back and ask your team, "How does the re-defined problem definition compare to my original problem or concern?" You may notice you get more clarity or different perspectives that can help refine the problem.

Let's take a deeper dive into this idea using an example of work we did around a portal testing tool, where our client wanted to procure an automation tool to streamline and standardize the execution of portal testing. After going through the empathize phase, developing personas and empathy maps, and looking at journey maps, they redefined the problem to include recording the results.

The element of test results was revealed after completing the empathize phase. So, rather than streamlining and standardizing the execution of portal testing, we changed the problem to reducing the time spent creating, executing, and recording test results.

The redefined challenge statement was more reflective of what they needed. It also provided vendors more clarity, brought clarity to the project's measures of success and priorities, and provided a clearer definition of the team's preferred outcome.

Design thinking is needed most for complex and chaotic challenges where there are unknown unknowns, and when you may not even know where to begin. It's important as we create the problem statement that we consider minimizing the chances of making bad decisions. The goal is to make the best decisions possible based on the evidence and information at hand. However, defining your challenge may take a few attempts.

Let's come back to our travel tool example. This was a complex environment which involved several departments across the country and lots of travel. The fact that more than 300,000 people would eventually use this system — and that it involved tight integration of policy, technology, people, and financial systems — only added to the complexity. To better understand the people involved, the team went across the country and across organizations.

As we gathered information about end users, we thought about the potential problem definition, and soon realized there might be an opportunity to redefine the problem: We weren't necessarily looking for a new system, but a way for people to book travel. This opened it up to the possibility that it didn't have to be a software system at all. There may have been an opportunity for people to book on their own outside a government-operated travel system.

Through this example, we can start to see how looking at actual needs can lead to solutions your team may not yet have considered.

Reframing the Problem to Gain New Insights

Reframing is an essential aspect of the design thinking process. Reframing is a strategic skill that enables your team to see a variety of fresh solutions to daunting challenges. By the end of this section, we'll understand how to reframe issues within your own team and with stakeholders, how to identify opportunities for reframing, as well as learn techniques for uncovering and eliminating assumptions that could hinder your team from finding the right solution.

Reframing is about keeping your ears and eyes open to doing things in a different way. It's mostly done during the final four phases of design thinking: Define, ideate, prototype, and test.

Remember — at its core, design thinking is about understanding end users to discover their real challenges. Reframing helps shed light on new angles of any issue from different perspectives. As we understand end users and their challenges, we can delve deeper into solution possibilities or consider incentives for end users to move to new solutions — not only helping us reframe, but helping our users reframe, as well.

Reframing involves thinking about the challenge at a higher level and getting to the core of what people want. We have all sorts of assumptions on what things are and how they're supposed to be, often without realizing it — and these assumptions can sometimes become mental barriers.

For example, years ago, a friend of mine asked me to go on vacation with her for the long weekend. She likes to travel so I assumed we'd jet off to Boston or New York, but she suggested Budapest. I automatically thought "no" because I assumed it would be too expensive for such a short trip. She then let me know that she found a deal on a flight and a reasonably priced Airbnb in a great location. Even though it was a good deal, I still felt I should say no. I couldn't think of a particular reason, and because I hadn't seen this friend in a long time, I agreed to go despite still feeling a little apprehensive.

It was only halfway through the trip that I realized I had an unconscious bias that European trips should be least seven days. Because of this mental framing around travelling, I was unconsciously looking for reasons not to go!

My friend helped me understand and push beyond this mental framing. In the end, the trip was phenomenal and we had a great time. This got me thinking about how I and others frame other aspects in our lives, like our work environments. The concept of thinking outside the box has become a bit cliché these days, but it's true that there are a lot of instances where we tend to have a certain way of thinking — sometimes to our detriment. Reframing helps us overcome these rigid perspectives and see challenges in new ways.

Assumptions are everywhere, after all: In our jobs, our projects, and our end users. What are your team's assumptions? Are there ways to check these assumptions?

Sometimes we have certain ideas about the way things are, or unconscious notions about the way things should be. Don't worry — everyone does this! What reframing does is help us ask ourselves, *"Who says* it has to always be that way?"* Asking that question helps break down the assumptions we've built.

Case in point: If we thought about a car 60 years ago, we would all have assumed it must run on gasoline. It probably wouldn't have a seat belt, and if it did, it wasn't commonly used. Fast forward to today and hybrid and electric cars are now commonplace. And seatbelts are a definite must!

As a society, we've reframed both grocery shopping and working from home a great deal recently. I used to think grocery shopping online would take longer and that I wouldn't get quality products or produce, but upon reframing my thinking around online grocery shopping, I found it is much more convenient for me most of the time!

Another example is how governments around the world have shifted how and where people can work, but there are other ways governments have used reframing.

For example, when the U.K. government looked at the tax payment system, the data showcased that a lot of people did not pay their taxes. And so, the *assumption* was made that people who didn't pay their taxes were doing so because they *didn't want* to pay them. But as the government spoke to residents they recognized that doing taxes was a very confusing process. Upon realizing this, they shifted their original assumption towards an understanding that people needed help filing their taxes. They realized they could simplify the process to help make it easier to file taxes — and, in turn, encourage more people to pay them.

Imagine how different this solution would be compared to the original challenge they thought they were trying to solve — the one where they thought people didn't want to pay taxes. All along, this original assumption had them trying to solve the wrong challenge. As a result of reframing, the solution they created was much different than if they had just stuck with their original assumption. And as the U.K. government rolled out new solutions, the rate of tax completion (and payment) increased.

We want to start by framing our challenge as a need. Let's look at Airbnb as an example.

Most people use this service when visiting other countries or cities. It is a way to find places to stay in the heart of the city and fills the gap when traditional accommodations aren't available or are fully booked. There's also Airbnb Experiences, which are activities hosted by local experts that can enhance your trip. These experiences help us reframe what we do when we travel and even in our own cities.

I remember an Airbnb excursion I went on in Colombia, where we stopped at a fruit stand on the side of the road. The guide — who took us there in his personal car — discussed the background of each fruit, along with the history and the politics of the area, while we sampled the stand's wares. Even being in the car helped us better understand the economics of the area: Roll-down windows, smaller vehicle sizes, no CD player, and definitely no Apple CarPlay!

We got to know the country better from the perspective of a local citizen and it made for a truly unique experience. We also felt we could trust the literature around this experience compared with other agencies, because Airbnb's ratings section contains reviews from other international travelers. Especially when travelling to a country where safety levels are different than one's home country, this aspect can make or break your trip.

What's most important is the incentive for reframing — people must want to do it. AirBnB provided lower costs, an authentic experience, availability, and an ability to see reviews from other travelers.

Reframing helps your team, on the other hand, see the problem as the outcome they want to create. Consider what your team is trying to do in terms of the outcome they want to have, as opposed to the output. Sometimes, when only outputs are top of mind, it gets in the way of the challenge we really need to solve.

Let's look at more reframing examples from the public sector.

We once worked with a team that had run into several issues during its last equipment procurement. The team also felt like the middleman between another department and the vendor, and didn't have the expertise to make decisions on what the vendor was asking of them.

We took the team through the design thinking process and, as the problem statement was developed, the team reframed their assumptions around purchasing physical technology to consider the possibility of opening it up to a managed solution (your team may think they need hardware or software, but may actually need a service instead).

Remember that the applications of reframing challenges are endless — whether it be in procurement, or in changing how policies or programs are run or executed. The possibilities for reframing are all around us!

Reframing is achieved by examining your limitations, or unconscious biases, based on your team's and the organization's beliefs and experiences. Looking at what your team thought about users and what the users said about themselves can provide new insights into how to solve challenges.

During the empathize phase, for example, we typically ask the core team working on the solution to develop personas of their end users. We then ask them to re-create these personas with the end users themselves. The team then compares both versions, to see the assumptions they may have made. This exercise is often very enlightening and provides opportunities to reframe where there might be biases.

You can also look to other organizations (or countries) for examples of reframing. For example, in 2016 Portugal wanted to increase civic participation among rural and remote citizens. The country sought to make budgetary voting more accessible for citizens in remote locations by enabling them to vote on budgetary proposals via ATMs (Automated Teller Machines). Portugal was able to reframe how voting was done: Instead of doing it at regular voting stations that might not be available in rural areas, they used ATMs available in these areas.

It's important to identify the ultimate root challenges so we can find opportunities for reframing. Portugal's root challenge was providing people in rural areas an opportunity to vote, and the opportunity was to create ways for citizens to vote in secure, non-traditional ways.

Be open to reframing by thinking how the challenge could be framed differently, and what incentives would encourage users to reframe. In other words: What's in it for them?

In our work within IT organizations, we've seen that most challenges aren't usually just an IT issue. Training, business process, data availability, and accuracy all come together as parts of most business challenges.

Design thinking allows and encourages your team to cast off preconceptions and use an evidence-based approach to defining and explaining what your team wants to accomplish.

In IT and other corporate functions, it's easy to understand the general problem space and build a complicated solution that does a lot of things but does not really fix the underlying issue.

Modern organizations increasingly focus on trying to assess business benefits rather than declaring victory if the project is on scope, on time, and on budget. There's an increased awareness of the need to design for the purposes of benefitting users.

The design thinking approach helps to not only identify direct user benefits but also longer-term organizational benefits, by capturing business problems in a language that users and executives recognize. Considering outcomes rather than outputs helps with this. Reframing allows your team to achieve the desired outcome while sometimes deviating from traditional outputs. It also leads to solutions that are better suited for users.

Recall a few pages earlier, one point of contact at an organization we worked with said something along the lines of: "There's no such thing as an IT project." What they meant by this is that business projects solve business problems, and IT may be just one tool to help make that happen. It's foolish to jump the gun and assume we know the exact scope at the start of a project. Design thinking forces us to approach the issue without presuming we know the answer.

Of course, knowing this is one thing — but having a toolkit to push us and our clients to approach the issue without presuming we know the answer is quite liberating, and leads to better outcomes.

Reframing might be new to your team or your organization, but the more your team does it, the easier it gets. The results can be phenomenal when your team has faith in the process.

The Five Whys

Before we get started on this section, let's go on a journey. We're travelling along the design thinking roadmap and have just come through the empathize phase with personas, empathy maps, journey maps and relevant data in hand. Now we're working our way through the define stage. Your team may have identified common or recurring issues and selected the challenges your team wants to solve. But how can your team be sure they're solving the right challenge?

Enter the five whys!

In this section we'll review what the five whys are, how they work, and when to use them in the design thinking process.

The five whys is a technique that will help your team further refine the challenge during the define stage of the design thinking process, allowing you to quickly dissect the problem and reveal its underlying causes.

The five whys is an iterative questioning technique used to explore the cause-and-effect relationships underlying a particular issue to determine its root cause. The five whys may show your team that the source of the issue isn't what you initially anticipated or defined, and that's okay!

For example, problems that are considered technical issues may turn out to be human and/or process issues instead, or as well as, technical issues.

Finding and eliminating the root cause of a challenge is crucial to determining the underlying solution and avoiding error or iteration at the define stage. The five whys are great for finding the root cause of the challenge you're trying to solve. Here are the steps:

- Define the problem you're trying to solve using other design thinking methods in the empathy stage
- Ask the first why — for example, why is problem X occurring?
- Ask why four more times to get to the root, or true cause of your challenge and solve from the bottom up!

Remember, conducting a five whys activity is useful during the define stage of the design thinking process, to help clarify and refine the challenge after identifying the problem you're looking to solve. The five whys are effective for resolving simple or moderately difficult challenges, like those you've narrowed down during the earlier stages of the design thinking process.

Here's an example of the five whys at work in the public sector when contracting and procurement challenges occur. The five whys was triggered to better understand if the challenge really was that contracting documents were too time consuming (which is what came out of empathizing with end users).

- Q1: Is production of contractual documents too time consuming? And if so, why?
  A: Yes, because the documents are overly complex and static.
- Q2: Why are the documents overly complex and static?
  A: Because clauses are written by legal professionals based on risk aversion and haven't been redesigned in 20 years to reflect procurement and technology changes.
- Q3: Why haven't clauses been redesigned for new procurement tactics and technology?
  A: Because procurement officers aren't measured on effectiveness or quality of contracts, and new tools and processes aren't valued.

- Q4: Why aren't new procurement tools and processes valued?
  A: Because there are numerous changes happening simultaneously and managers are measured on the creation of new tools, not their adoption or uptake, which leads to no maintenance plan for new tools and processes.
- Q5: Why aren't maintenance plans in place for new tools and processes?
  A: Because leaders and executives don't know how to handle innovation at a working level, and prefer to handle it at a corporate level, but corporate-level executives aren't familiar with procurement.
- Q6: Why isn't the corporate level focusing on this?
  A: Because procurement officers aren't given ownership over the contracting process.

This approach helped get at the solution: To enhance leadership roles at the corporate level to overhaul and oversee the procurement process and create maintenance plans for new tools. These roles should be held by people who understand the procurement process and take ownership in simplifying the process for suppliers.

The five whys could also be used around hiring and retaining new employees. One of our clients contacted us to identify what they could do to retain new employees that were also new postsecondary graduates. Here's how we used the five whys with the participants to approach how they could solve their challenge:

- Q1: Why are our new grads leaving within two years of joining the organization?
  A: Because they don't feel like they're having an impact.
- Q2: Why don't they feel like they're having an impact?
  A: Because they don't feel connected to other people or to their projects.

- Q3: Why don't they feel connected?
  A: Because they don't get asked for their opinions or thoughts — they are just told what to do without explanation of how their work fits in with everything else or the bigger picture.
- Q4: Why aren't they being asked for their thoughts?
  A: Because people feel like they have too much to do already and don't take the time to ask or connect.
- Q5: Why don't they have enough time?
  A: Because there aren't enough resources available to do the work.

The solution here: Spend time asking new team members their thoughts and bring them fully into the team, including explaining how their work fits into the bigger picture so they understand, are engaged, and want to stay.

Tip 1: Five isn't always the magic number
In some cases, your team may need to ask why more than five times to get to the root cause of the issue, or your team may reach this point before the fifth why.

Tip 2: Know when to stop
The most important thing is to know when to stop asking why. It's when your questions stop producing useful responses.

Fishbone Diagrams

To solve the defined challenge effectively, your team needs to determine the underlying cause or causes of your challenge. That's where a fishbone diagram comes in handy!

We'll review what fishbone diagrams are, how to make one, when to use them in the design thinking process, along with an example and an activity.

Fishbone or Ishikawa diagrams are causal diagrams that show the potential cause of a specific event.

Some may recognize them from project management courses, as they often use fishbone diagrams to define the root cause of issues. To create a fishbone diagram:

- Write the problem statement in a box to one side of your page (this is the fish head)
- From the fish head, draw a line from left to right. This is the spine of your fish
- Draw fish bones emanating from the spine, which represent the main cause categories. Label each fish bone with a category title
- Brainstorm all causes that relate to the problem statement
- Keep in mind that any issue can fall in several categories
- Each individual on your team then uses supporting data to decide on the top three causes as they see them
- Select the top three causes with the highest scores. These three issues will now form the basis of additional investigation to find the root cause

For the main cause categories we use generic category labels such as people, method, technology, material, and environment. Or we brainstorm major cost categories related to the specific problem.

Your team can investigate these causes further using design thinking tools like the five whys. Fishbone diagrams are used during the define stage of the design thinking process to analyze a complex problem that has multiple causes. They're also used for identifying all possible root causes of a particular problem.

Let's work through an example together. In this example, we want to increase the efficiency of the production of contractual documents:

- First, we drew a blank fishbone diagram. For the main cause categories we used a mix of generic category labels and major cost categories related to increased efficiency of the production of contracted documents.
- Next, we drew a horizontal line from our fish head or problem statement to form our fish spine.
- Next, we brainstormed the causes related to the challenge and added them under their respective categories. An issue can fall into several categories. For example, in the process category, we've added decision-makers and the decision-making process, industry consultation, and selecting the appropriate clause. The same process was then done for the technology, people, policy and regulation, and procurement categories.
- Team members selected their top three causes.
- We then considered the insights garnered from the fishbone diagram.

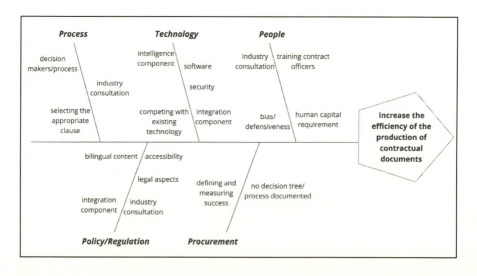

Now we know what a fishbone diagram is, and when and how to use one in the design thinking process to further refine the challenge during the define stage.

Mind Maps

We mentioned mind maps a few times earlier in the chapter. If your team is in the define stage of the design thinking process and needs to identify the challenge that needs to be solved, mind maps are a great tool. In this section we'll review what mind maps are, how to use them, when to use them in the design thinking process, along with an example and an activity.

A mind map is a diagram used to visually organize information. Mind maps are a great way to showcase and analyze data non-linearly, and allow us to easily identify connections, commonalities, and other group-like elements.

Mind maps are used during the define phase of the design thinking process to help identify challenges. They can also be used during the ideate phase to brainstorm potential solutions.

To create a mind map, start by writing the challenge — or area you want to expand on — in the center of your page. Add any related topics around your initial statement. Continue branching out from these related topics to identify sub-branches or subtopics.

It's up to your team to decide exactly how mind maps are created. You can use online applications like we did for the previous map, or tools your team already has, such as PowerPoint. Or you can do it the old-fashioned way and create maps by hand.

Let's now look at a mind map example with our persona, Andrew, the manager from the empathize chapter. Here's a mind map of Andrew's challenges around working from home, such as space, convenience, and technology, along with related elements such as limited access to his team, no home office, distractions, internet issues, and the commute.

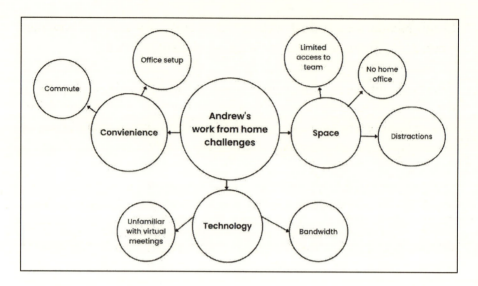

We often use mind maps during the define stage of the design thinking process to help determine the challenge we need to solve. But mind maps can also be useful during the ideate stage when brainstorming potential solutions.

Use mind maps to dig deeper into your challenges or ideas. Consider what insights mind maps provide. Is your team able to see connections they might not have seen before? Note if some elements occur more frequently than others.

Entity, Relationships, Attributed and Flow (ERAF) System Diagram

In this section, we'll look at entities, relationships, attributes, and flow (ERAF) system diagrams.

We've reached the define stage of the design thinking process and need to determine the challenge or challenges to solve. As your team defines the challenges, it's important to analyze the current processes and connections to determine where issues arise. This is where ERAF system diagrams come in handy.

In this section we'll look at what ERAF system diagrams are, how they work, and when to use them in the design thinking process.

ERAF system diagrams are used during the define phase of the design thinking process to visually understand the components and connections of a system. They can also be used during the prototyping phase to visually represent a solution.

The components of an ERAF system diagram include the entities, people, places, and things within a system, along with the relationships between entities, their attributes, and the flow or direction of actions between entities. This example shows entities' relationships, attributes, and flows within the system of onboarding employees in the public sector.

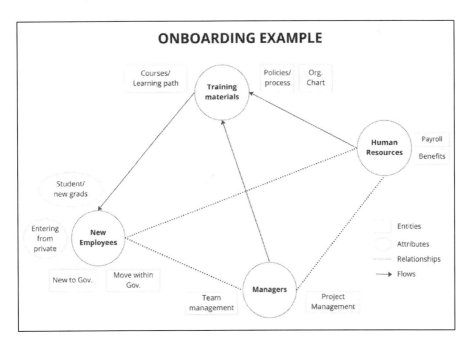

We show the entities of new employees, training materials, managers, and human resources, with dotted lines showing the relationships between these entities and arrows showing flow of information. We also include the attributes of each of these entities, including new employees, those new to government, or those working within government.

Government work often includes several interconnected systems, and ERAF diagrams can help visualize all these systems working together.

Consider the insights the diagram provides. Now we know what ERAF system diagrams are, and when and how to use them in the design thinking process when defining your challenge or displaying prototypes.

Design Thinking in Action: The Passport Application, Part 2

In the previous chapter we highlighted Stevie's challenges and pain points throughout their passport renewal journey. The next step is defining Stevie's main challenge by reframing the initial challenge and using a combination of mind mapping and HMW (How might we) techniques.

We learned about Stevie's challenges from the persona, empathy map, and journey map stages of the empathize phase. These are shown in the mind map below. From this mind map we can define the primary challenge and frame it using the HMW technique, as shown below. The client's problem is that they are unaware of the status of their application. The HMW technique helps reframe this as: How might we inform the applicants of their application status?

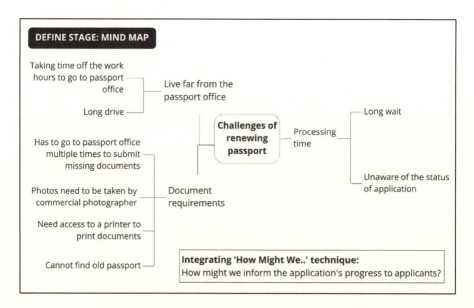

DEFINE STAGE: MIND MAP

Taking time off the work hours to go to passport office

Live far from the passport office

Long drive

Challenges of renewing passport

Processing time

Long wait

Has to go to passport office multiple times to submit missing documents

Photos need to be taken by commercial photographer

Document requirements

Unaware of the status of application

Need access to a printer to print documents

Cannot find old passport

Integrating 'How Might We..' technique:
How might we inform the application's progress to applicants?

Summary — Define Phase

In the second step of the design thinking process, we learned to:

- Define the problem
  - o Digging deep to uncover and understand the real challenge

- Create a problem statement
  - o Providing clarity and conciseness to the problem for those involved in the design process

- Reframe the problem
  - o Gaining new insights by challenging assumptions and identifying ideal outcomes

- Use tools to further explore the root causes of the challenge
  - o The five whys, fishbone diagrams, and mind maps

By the end of the define phase, you have synthesized the information uncovered in the empathize phase to articulate your challenge in a clearly defined problem statement. The end user's perspective has continued to be considered, and assumptions have been challenged. Taking the time to thoughtfully consider all perspectives at this stage will enable you to move on to the next phases with confidence, knowing the underlying issue that you are working to solve.

You'll end up referring to your defined problem statement throughout the remainder of the design thinking process. Think of it as your project's magnetic north. This helps you know you are on track to solve the right challenge for your users.

Step 3: Ideate

Introduction to Ideation

Now that we've identified the initial problem and measures of success, empathized with end users, and gone through the define phase, we are now ready to begin the ideate phase (also called the ideation phase) of the design thinking roadmap.

This is probably the most fun part of design thinking — coming up with ideas! We can get creative juices flowing during the ideation phase with brainstorming, collaborating, and hackathons.

In this chapter, we'll talk about how to run high-level ideation sessions and discuss co-creation.

We'll look at ideation and brainstorming at a high level. It's helpful to understand several techniques so your team can use whatever best suits your challenge and audience, and we often find that different techniques bring forward new and different ways of solving problems. Different techniques bring out different creative aspects of our brains. We'll also discuss how to narrow down ideas and select ideas to move to the next phase.

The ideate or ideation phase is where your teams identify solutions to the challenges identified in the define stage. This is where we generate ideas as we incorporate a wide variety of perspectives and ideas, which is why some call this the brainstorming stage. It's about generating ideas that can be prototyped in the next step. We want to gather as much divergent thinking as possible from a wide variety of perspectives so we can come up with unexpected ideas, and we do this by assembling a group, with or without end clients, to come up with potential ideas and ways to solve the problem.

In innovation and creativity, we often hear the term "think outside the box" — but if things are too out there, most people can't see the value because it is just too different. The best way to come up with great ideas is to come up with a bunch of good ideas and build on them.

The box is important, though, because it's on the edges where we have leverage. We need to nail down what the box is before we can create something that's seen as creative. That's why ideation is about coming up with as many ideas as possible, both inside and around the edges of the box, as well as outside the box. What's either in or outside the box depends on the organization and its leader's sensitivities and mindset to develop a more modern and transformative organization.

Creating Psychological Safe Zones

How do we ideate? We like to co-create with end users by bringing users and stakeholders into the solving-the-problem phase. To successfully co-create it's important to focus on the challenge at hand, rather than thinking about it as us-vs-them. We want to create a safe environment for co-creation where knowledge is shared and there's an open discussion. This involves creating psychological safe zones.

A psychological safe zone is a space — it doesn't have to be a physical space — where people feel like they're all on the same level, devoid of hierarchy, and are free to share thoughts and ideas as humans without fear of being judged, reprimanded, or criticized.

One of the best ways to get people into psychological safe zones is to first get them out of their comfort zone, as this is when people are more open to new ideas and to learning from others. It doesn't have to be extreme — just slight changes from how people normally work and think are often enough. There are different ways to get people out of their comfort zones that may initially make them uncomfortable, but that's kind of the point — it gets them geared up to be in a more open, creative mindset moving forward. If people typically write at work, try things like drawing or sketching, for example.

Brainstorming Techniques

Coming up with ideas involves brainstorming, either individually or in teams (we focus on brainstorming in teams in this section). Because brainstorming and ideation is one of the most fun and interesting parts of design thinking, sometimes we don't even realize we're brainstorming. This phase of design thinking allows us to pull back and take the time to create environments and opportunities for many people to provide ideas, thoughts, and perspectives.

Many organizations have one or two techniques as their go-to brainstorming techniques. The most common approach we see is the blank page technique, where people get together and put down as many ideas as possible on a blank sheet. This works!

But there are ways to help enhance the ideas and types of ideas the team comes up with. These are jumping-off points to help solve the problem. We recommend trying two or more different types of brainstorming techniques to get an even greater variety and breadth of ideas.

This is a capture of the whiteboarding technique done virtually with end users. This a list of ideas.

Challenge: The impacted employees do not understand the change

Potential solutions:

- Encourage them to reach out to contacts for more information - union rep, managers, colleagues
- Encourage them to provide a list of items they don't understand (i.e. questions)
- Provide them with a sense of the process (ex. timelines, next steps)
- Create a web page with all the information
- Offer question and answer sessions
- Provide them with supplementary information such as org. chart so they can understand the bigger picture of the change (i.e. new org. structure)
- Review the job description together as a group
- Involve an early adopter/influencer to help with some of the options
- Walk them through how it impacts them in more operational details (ex. how they will be able to do the new duties)

This illustrates how ideation can happen virtually in a format people are used to — the written word. But there are so many great tools out there for ideation. It's not just about using words — drawings and pictures can sometimes help convey and develop ideas even better than words can.

As with all brainstorming techniques, look to build on one another's ideas whenever possible. Leave the critiquing and judging out. This is the time to throw everything into the light of day. Building on one another's ideas can help increase the number and quality of the original ideas.

Often, all that's needed to get started is a simple **icebreaker**. As an exercise, we often have one of the participants in the brainstorming session start with a sentence, then go around the room and have each person build on the previous sentence to create a story or enhance an idea. This is sometimes referred to an improv icebreaker. This requires participants to listen very carefully to those before them. Feel free to go around the room as many times as you want.

Gap filling, mind map, challenger, and resource availability are my favourite types of brainstorming techniques. They're simple to do with any audience and don't require much time.

- **Gap filling.** You're at point A, and you know you want to get to point B. So, what's the gap that exists between A and B? What do you need to bridge this gap?
- **Mind map.** We discussed this technique in a previous section. Add as many ideas as you can in hierarchical tree and cluster format — your central issue is in the middle, and then the ideas create sub-branches.
- **Challenger.** List all the assumptions in your situation and challenge them (we'll discuss shortly in more detail).
- **Resource availability.** What if money, time, people, supplies weren't limiting factors? What if you could ask for — and receive — whatever you want? What could we create? This one can be pretty phenomenal, as it's amazing what we can come up with when we don't limit ourselves. We can then work backwards to reverse engineer how much of that idea we can create in real life. Spoiler alert: It's often a lot more than we initially thought.

All four of the techniques above are great. But my all-time favorite brainstorming technique is probably reverse thinking.

Reverse thinking involves thinking about what most people would typically do in your situation, then doing the opposite. For senior citizen personas at a coffee shop, think about the type of environment that would not be ideal for them — loud music, dim lighting, no room to sit. This leads to discovering that lighting is something designers can use to make the experience better for this persona.

In a public sector environment, this might mean looking at senior citizens in a service office scenario. What would not be ideal for them? In terms of digital displays in a service center, this probably would include things like too-small print, pages changing too quickly, the screen being too bright, not enough contrast, and too many options on the screen.

We use many more types of brainstorming techniques. Let's learn more about them:

- **The time travel technique** is about looking at how you'd deal with a challenge if you were in a different era. Ten years ago? How about in the future? Ten years later?

- **Attribute change** is about how you would think about the issue if you were a different gender, age, education, height, nationality — anything. With each attribute change, you become exposed to a different spectrum of thinking.

- Another favourite brainstorming technique our team loves is thinking about what you'd do if you were someone else? This is also known as **rolestorming**. For example: Your manager? Minister or prime minister? President? Partner? Your best friend? Your enemy? The list goes on.

- **The iconic figures technique** is a spinoff of rolestorming. What if you were an iconic figure of the past? Buddha? Albert Einstein? Thomas Edison? Marie Curie? Winston Churchill? Nelson Mandela? How about the present? Oprah Winfrey? Elon Musk? Richard Branson? Joe Biden? How would they handle the situation?

- **Brain writing**. Get a group of people and have them write their ideas on their own sheet of paper. After 10 minutes, rotate sheets to different people and build from what the others wrote. Continue until everyone has written on everyone else's paper.

- **The trigger method** means brainstorming as many ideas as possible. Then select the best ones and brainstorm on those ideas as triggers for more ideas. Repeat until you find the best solution.

- **Variable brainstorming** involves identifying the variable in the outcome you want. For example, if your goal is to achieve X number of applicants to your program, the variable is the number of applicants. Start by listing all the possibilities for that variable. Different variations are gender, age, nationality, regionality, occupation, interests, tech savviness, and education. Think about the question with each variable. For example, for gender: How can you get more females to apply to your program? For age: How can you get more teenagers applying to your program? And so on.

- **Exaggeration**. Exaggerate your goal to determine how you'll deal with it now. Enlarge it: What if it's 10 times its current size? 100 times? Or shrink it: What if it's one-tenth its current size?
- The last brainstorming technique is to write a **list of 101 ideas** to deal with your situation. Go wild and write whatever you can think of without restricting your team. Don't stop until you have at least 101 ideas.

These techniques are just the tip of the iceberg. We have lots more ways of ideating depending on your need and situation.

Different techniques work with different personalities and environments. Introverts may prefer something like brainwriting, where participants write down their ideas but aren't singled out. An extrovert, on the other hand, may prefer taking turns voicing their ideas and thoughts in an activity like rolestorming.

As we mentioned earlier, some loose rules and guidelines around brainstorming include:

- Go for quantity, not quality
- Defer judgement and don't censor ideas
- All ideas are good ideas
- Build on each other's ideas
- Encourage crazy ideas — think improvisation at a comedy club

Just a reminder that if you have constraints that have been validated as constraints (rather than assumptions disguised as constraints), it may be worthwhile discussing these with your co-creators as your team comes up with ideas together. It's super important to verify that these are true constraints, however. Oftentimes we think things are constraints because of what we've been taught, but upon further investigation, it may be hard to show that it really is a constraint.

We want to avoid constraining as much as possible, but — especially in the public sector — there may be regulations, laws, and rules in place that can't be changed in the immediate future. There are other things that are also hard to change like departmental policy and union rules. It's important to let your co-creators know about these as they're brainstorming.

Have your entire team participate in brainstorming sessions. Also consider asking your clients to join. Frequently the people who have the challenge — your clients — have ideas on how they'd like issues solved, and their ideas may surprise you.

Hackathons are another way of group brainstorming. Hackathons are good for more than developing code. They're usually done in public settings where a question or a challenge is posed to groups of people. Teams come up with potential solutions to the problem, then prototype them. We've been involved with several hackathons with the public sector, the private sector, and academia, and it's always amazing to see the diversity of ideas that come forward.

There are techniques and methods to help determine which ideas to take to the prototype phase, which we'll discuss in later sections. This is like how we selected our redefined challenge, and can be applied here as well, whether you go with voting, looking for common themes, or mapping it on ERAF diagrams.

Either way, when selecting ideas to prototype, always make sure they will solve the challenge. It's easy to get wrapped up coming up with great ideas but then lose track of why we're coming up with those ideas in the first place. Always ensure the ideas you select to prototype will address the redefined problem.

Your team's constraints and timelines may play a role here, as well. It's great to have a vision of what the team wants in the long term for the project (such as a five-year vision), but if you only have 12 months to create a solution, or part of the solution, you need to select ideas that fit those constraints while still working on long-term goals.

The challenger is another good brainstorming technique.

How does the challenger technique work? It's very simple. First, list all assumptions about your situation. Then challenge them. The challenger is used during the ideate phase of the design thinking process to determine the accuracy of your assumptions.

For example, one of our clients' goals was to sell her art online. But the first assumption was the online element: Why did it need to be sold online? Could it be sold in a gallery? Could she sell it in a decor store?

The second assumption was around display: Did it need to be still images? Could she create videos of the art? New ideas came to mind such as displaying the art in restaurants, cafes, and other business spaces. She explored options like using an online platform, such as an Instagram page instead of a traditional website, or having online influencers promote the work.

Challenging assumptions can lead to new or different ideas and ways of thinking about challenges. In our art example, it may generate new ideas around medium, decoration, and display. It's up to your team how much time to spend challenging assumptions, but always ensure your team records all the results that emerge from any challenger sessions.

In another example, a team we worked with wanted to brainstorm ideas for an online procurement portal being rolled out department-wide to improve procurement. The team's first assumption was around technology: An online portal. Does it need to be an online portal? Could it be a different format? Their second assumption was around people:

Does the team know that people want to or can use an online portal? Is there another service format they may prefer? This process may lead to new delivery ideas the team hadn't thought of previously.

A third example involves brainstorming solutions to allow your team to hire faster. The first assumption is that hiring takes a long time. Does it? How long does it take? What aspects of the process take the most time?

The second assumption is that your team must follow the same process used in the past. How do we know which aspects of the process are necessary? Using the challenger technique here could lead to a list of solutions to hire faster, such as an expedited hiring process or a review of the current process to determine what can be eliminated. It can also help identify if the process is actually slow or just perceived as slow: What are the industry standards? What are other organizations doing?

Oftentimes there are a lot of assumptions when working in a large, ever-changing system or organization like the public sector — and sometimes these assumptions are inaccurate.

Think about your team's current situation and the assumptions they have. What additional ideas can your team come up with after challenging your assumptions?

Entity Position Maps

As your team co-creates potential solutions with your end users, how do you know which solutions to prototype and test? An entity position map is one tool that can help narrow it down. In this section we'll cover what entity position maps are, how they work, and when to use them in the design thinking process.

An entity position map correlates entities in relation to two relevant project parameters. Typically part of the ideation phase, entity position maps can synthesize the great ideas from the ideation phase and determine their viability before moving to the prototype phase.

Entity maps typically contain the project parameters you want to compare, such as time vs. cost or time vs. impact.

In this example, we've compared the time and cost it would take to implement more effective work-from-home solutions. We've set the time it takes to implement a solution as short, medium, or long term, and determined if the cost to implement each solution would be above or below budget.

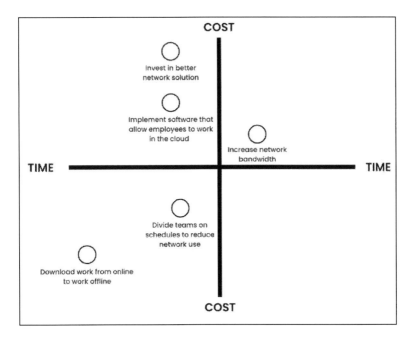

As the diagram shows, investing in a better network solution may be a relatively quick solution, but it has a high price tag. Alternatively, allowing employees to download documents and work offline is a cost-effective solution in the short term.

A fun way to provide perspective is to do entity position maps on the floor, using colored tape to denote the axis, then using objects in the room to plot out the points. For example, to illustrate the point on dividing teams by schedules to reduce network use, use a clock.

Entity position maps identify, or at least narrow down, ideas from the ideation phase to help you move to the next phase of design thinking — prototyping.

Design Thinking in Action: The Passport Application, Part 3

Back to our passport application example. The main challenge was identified in Part 2, and now the next step is to generate ideas to address the issue. To achieve this a spinoff of rolestorming is used below, with Amazon as our reference company.

What if we had capabilities and technology comparable to Amazon? How might we inform the applicant of their application's progress? By using this brainstorming technique we can more easily come up with ideas for solutions, and then choose two of them for prototyping.

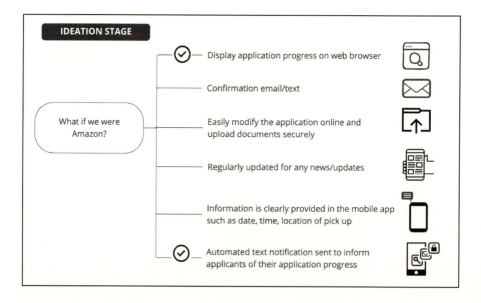

Summary — Ideate Phase

In the third step of the design thinking process, we covered:

- How to ideate effectively
    - Forming an environment that encourages creativity and co-creation between end-users and stakeholders

- Brainstorming
    - Techniques and guidelines to bring out a variety of ideas and perspectives for consideration

- How to select the best ideas
    - Entity position maps synthesize the best ideas and determine which solutions will proceed to prototyping and testing

In the ideation phase, we have collectively brainstormed with relevant stakeholders and end users to discover potential solutions for our defined problem. We've learned that using different brainstorming techniques that fit with the personalities and environment you work with will help generate a wide variety of ideas.

After ensuring that all ideas, thoughts, and perspectives have been heard and considered, the most viable solutions for solving our end users' challenge can be identified. Constraints, timelines, and entity positioning are additional aspects to consider when narrowing down solutions.

The selected solutions will next move onto the two remaining phases of the design thinking process — prototyping and testing.

Step 4: Prototype

Introduction to Prototyping

Welcome to prototyping, the fourth phase in the design thinking process. During prototyping you'll take your ideas from ideation to the real world. In this chapter, we'll cover how your team can build on ideas and gain further insights from users as they test your prototypes. We'll also discuss how this highly important phase helps de-risk innovation by allowing you to move from iteration to iteration quickly — and how it keeps your team from spending time and money on the wrong solutions. Let's jump right in!

Prototyping helps sustain momentum and focus, forcing your team to consider the initial input and design open-ended solutions. Design thinking is about providing options to our users, and the prototyping phase is where this starts to take form.

There are different ways to prototype. Essentially there are two types of prototypes — **high fidelity and low fidelity**. A high-fidelity prototype is one that's close to the final version. In design thinking, we mostly focus on low-fidelity prototyping which is less refined.

Remember that design thinking is about understanding end users' needs to discover their real issues.

The prototyping phase is another opportunity for us to understand these needs by building prototypes and getting user input. This is a great opportunity to keep our eyes and ears open to doing things in a different way. Until this point, we've begun to understand our end users and their challenges through the empathize phase, which involved defining their problems and coming up with ideas. During the prototyping phase we'll select the best ideas to move forward so we can build real-world versions of those concepts.

Prototyping is also about understanding end users better and looking for solutions, even after one has been found, to provide options. You may not always get your first prototype right on the first try — and that's okay! It's all part of the prototyping phase.

Prototyping is actually quite simple. We do it all the time in our personal lives, from trying a new route to get home or testing a new banana bread recipe. It helps to recognize how and when we prototype, so that it makes it easier to prototype in our work environment.

It's important to prime your mindset for prototyping. First, understand that not only is it okay to prototype, but it's imperative that you do so.

It's also important to realize (and even embrace) the reality that not everything you try is going to succeed. Your team might develop prototypes that your end users don't like, and in those cases it's important to regroup and review. If it doesn't succeed there are ways to get out of it. This is part of the process. Remember: It's just a first pass.

Even if users don't like your prototypes, getting this feedback is crucial. Prototyping is about getting more information on your ideas and end users. The mindset for prototyping, like the empathize phase, should be rooted in curiosity about your end users — not necessarily rooted in getting it right the first time.

Types of Prototyping

Earlier in the chapter we mentioned two types of prototypes: High fidelity and low fidelity. Each of these types has various prototyping subtypes. We'll discuss six different kinds of prototypes below.

1. Proof-of-principle. These prototypes verify key functions of the intended design. An example of this in a security software environment is Winzapper, a tool used to delete events from the Windows Security Log. This simple program demonstrated that once an administrator account has been compromised, event logs are no longer reliable. As a proof-of-principle it possessed the minimum capabilities needed to selectively remove an item from the Windows Security Log, but was not optimized in any other way.

2. User experience. These prototypes are meant to be used with human interaction. They represent enough of the appearance and function of the products or services that they can be used for user research purposes. User experience can be applied to many things, from applications or websites to services, processes, policies and programs. In the public sector, if we're looking to change a process and have two prototypes of that process, walking users through both to determine which they prefer is the user experience method of prototyping.

Both types of prototypes can be either high or low fidelity, depending on your needs, where you are in your research, and other available resources. Other prototyping types include:

3. Working prototypes. These typically include nearly all the functionality of a finished product. This prototype version is likely to be high fidelity. The National Research Council of Canada (NRC) has a wind tunnel that is used by organizations and businesses to test prototypes of plans, buildings, and vehicles — including NASCAR vehicles and their aerodynamic properties.

4. Functional prototypes. These capture both the function and appearance of the intended design. Functional prototypes may be created with different techniques and scale from the final design. An example of a functional prototype is a mock-up of a website using Figma UX software. Figma allows you to create the screens of each webpage with almost exact accuracy, including transitions and links to demonstrate functionality.

In most cases the latter two types would most likely be high-fidelity prototypes, as they come close to what the finished product would look like. Especially in these examples, functional and working prototypes can take time and effort to build.

5. Visual prototypes. These have the same size and appearance but not the intended functionality of the finished product. These could be sketches, cardboard models, or foam models emphasizing the geometric features of the design.

6. Paper prototypes. These are printed or hand-drawn representations of the user interface, or the product, process, or even policy. This is my favorite kind of prototype (especially during the low-fidelity phase) because it conveys ideas to others in a simple, inexpensive way. It's fascinating how much more input we get from our testers when our prototypes are in draft mode. People are much more comfortable commenting and making suggestions for improvement when something looks to be in its early stages.

Here's an example of a paper prototype:

The key to prototyping is that the design should showcase your ideas to end users so that you can get their input on what they like (and don't like).

Your team can prototype anything — including processes, services, products, documents, or regulations. Some techniques we recommend are storyboards, wireframes, or models. We cover both storyboards and wireframes in more detail later in this chapter.

How to Prototype

The key takeaway for prototyping is that there are methods and techniques that can help make the process easier, but prototype in any way that works best for your team. Your prototypes just need to showcase the capabilities your team wants to test.

Let's talk about an example from Canadian Blood Services (CBS), the manager of the country's blood supply, which prototyped different layouts of its donation facilities to improve the donor experience.

The initial model was a taped layout where users could interact with the facility environment. Users could move through the facilities so the team could observe what was working well and what wasn't in the physical layout.

The organization made a concerted effort to understand donors' needs and tried to make the blood donation experience as pleasant as possible by adjusting their facility layout. This illustrates the importance of taking time to develop strong prototypes and solutions with end users whenever possible.

There's a lot of different tools and software that can be used for prototyping. We often use pencil and paper and whiteboards. In the virtual world a variety of free whiteboard software, can be used such as Google Jamboards, Miro, IdeaBoardz, Mural, Figma, Padlet, Sketchbox, or Microsoft PowerPoint.

Kids often use software such as Sketch or Thunkable for prototyping games and applications. There's nothing stopping your team from using these or similar tools to ideate and prototype!

So, how many prototypes does your team need? We recommend starting with two. Offering too many prototypes can make it hard to differentiate during testing. Keep in mind your team can have several prototypes running for different parts of a service or product at the same time.

Some organizations may not be comfortable with multiple prototypes. During in-person training, when we ask our clients to create two prototypes, most spend much of their time on one prototype and feel it is perfect. When we ask them to create another one, they're sometimes a bit hesitant. But after they create their second prototype, they often end up liking it much more than the first! And it often takes even less time to create.

Developing prototypes is about creating space for different options for end users, and about understanding end users better. Remember this is an iterative process — once your team creates prototypes and tests them, they may find they need to re-iterate the prototype and test phases.

Your team can prototype anything. For example, your team can prototype two different ways of showcasing questions being asked or develop a different communication template to use at each phase of the process. Your team can do this several ways — either through email, surveys, or with PowerPoint presentations.

The key is trying to better understand end users and embracing the opportunity to create prototypes with end users. Let's discuss that in more detail now.

Creating prototypes with end users enables your team to discover what they like and don't like about the solution. Ask users how they'd like to have their challenges solved.

For example, with the travel systems project, we had users develop prototypes — and we got LOTS of prototypes from the teams involved. The team leading the project went across Canada to talk to and collaborate with users in the regions and received a large number of varying prototypes. We were then able to test some of the prototypes with end users.

In one of the sessions, we had around 100 participants. We grouped them into teams and asked them to create and test multiple prototypes with others in the room to get reactions to the prototypes right then and there! We work with many organizations that must renew, recreate, refresh, or create systems, tools, processes, regulations, and more. It's fascinating to see how often systems are created for past needs. This means resources are spent on past challenges, while the current challenges or those coming down the pipe aren't addressed.

Sometimes the challenge for people is that they can only think of incremental changes or shifts. Sometimes they need extra help to see the art of the possible. Some people instinctively try to solve smaller challenges, rather than think systematically about how it could be completely re-thought and reframed.

For example, in one of our engagements, the team was tasked to recreate a system (with a lot of freedom and support to determine what that meant). The current system was introduced more than 20 years ago — and while some improvements were made over time, no one ever really liked the system. So, instead of working on a new IT system no one would like for the next 20 years, they took the time to understand why the system wasn't liked, what people needed, and what their challenges were while using the system. They recognized the importance of having a deep understanding of the end user context to anticipate future needs.

To understand these future needs it's often crucial to prime people's brains. If you've worked in an organization for a long time, it's more likely you'll come up with incremental changes unless you spend time priming your brain. This means thinking about current services and technologies out there, both in our personal and professional lives, and extending that thinking to your environment.

If it's the public sector, we can show what other public sector organizations are doing or what they have planned for the future. We can ask: "What do you see the environment looking like in five years?" Oftentimes, the solutions we're looking at could take a year (or two, sometimes) to implement.
That's why it's key to get people to think about not just today's needs, but tomorrow's as well.

Now we'll look at different ways the public sector does prototyping. First is an example of a pilot project run by a Canadian provincial government seeking to increase the uptake of organ donation registration. It turned out that the organ donation registration form was usually given to citizens while updating their driver's licence in-person at service centres.

Citizens were unprepared to complete the lengthy and cumbersome form while visiting the centre. This meant that forms often weren't completed, leading to low uptake.

The province found enormous success through prototyping and learning more about how users interacted with the process. The project team tested a few different ways of increasing donor registration based on the principles of behavioural insights.

- One prototype provided different versions of the organ donor registration form
- One involved changing the timing of when the form was handed out
- The last one offered additional donor information to help people make their decision

The project team tested a couple different conditions involving giving citizens a simplified registration form when arriving at the service centre. As citizens waited they could read the information pamphlet and decide to complete the form. According to *Smith Magazine*[6] this was a resounding success: Organ donation registration increased by 143 percent at the service centre that held the testing.

Our next example comes from one of our clients at a Canadian municipality. Their team wanted to increase uptake of a program meant to improve residential infrastructure, to comply with health and safety standards. By examining citizen behaviour, the team determined the types of individuals that would most likely interact (and therefore take advantage of the program) based on their comfort level with technology. The team created personas based on how people interacted with the city — either digitally or in person — which helped them develop prototypes. They ended up creating both paper-based and digital prototype program intake forms and tested each format for feasibility.

Another example is from a client organization looking to change the perception of the nuclear industry. Their prototypes were a series of documentary-style videos describing the role of safety inspectors at nuclear sites. The purpose was to make additional information available to educate the public and demonstrate the work of nuclear industry professionals. In one version of the videos, the team used Lego characters and pieces to depict the facility inspector and other personnel typically found on-site. The videos' narration described what an inspector does at the site. All these prototyped videos were a few minutes long and were shared by participants on their smartphones to gain feedback quickly and easily.

At the onset of this stage, it's important to think about how your team will build the prototype. What materials will your team need? What is your team testing for? What does your team want to measure or observe? It's always fun to try prototypes with end users, but never lose sight of your team's goals.

In addition to this, ask your team: "How does what we're testing for align with our measures of success for this project?" If successful, will your team's prototypes meet the team's measures of success?

Prototyping is another great opportunity to test the assumptions your team made earlier. As your team develops the prototype, keep in mind they're also trying to meet the measures of success while either ruling out or verifying your team's earlier assumptions.

As your team prototypes, ask them if the prototypes meet the refined challenge. It helps to think back to the define phase, where we took what we learned from our end users and redefined the challenge based on their true needs. We must check these needs again as we prototype to make sure what we've built addresses the re-defined challenge, and if it can meet our measures of success.

It's easy to get excited about ideas and prototypes, but you must always come back to your magnetic north:

Developing solutions to your users' challenges. Before going into full-blown implementations, at the prototype phase it's vital to constantly ask your team, "Will our prototypes meet these needs?"

Remember that in the design thinking process, prototyping is about understanding end users better, seeing what works, and adapting based on those insights. It's an opportunity to see and hear things we may not have seen or heard before.

Storyboards and Wireframes

Whether your team prototypes a process, product, or service, a storyboard or wireframe is an effective way to visualize the steps and user experience of your solution. In this section, we'll review what storyboards and wireframes are, how they're used, and when to use them in the design thinking process.

A storyboard is a visual representation of a process or sequence that breaks actions down into individual panels. Storyboards are used to convey a process or service visually and sequentially, and are often used in marketing to create marketing funnels and commercials.

Let's come back to our passport renewal example. Once your team determines the idea they wish to prototype, define the scenes or stages of the process or service and add drawings or icons to visually represent each phase.

In this next example we've used icons to represent downloading the passport application form, filling out the application form, gathering your references, getting a passport photo taken, submitting the completed form to Service Canada, and providing payment details.

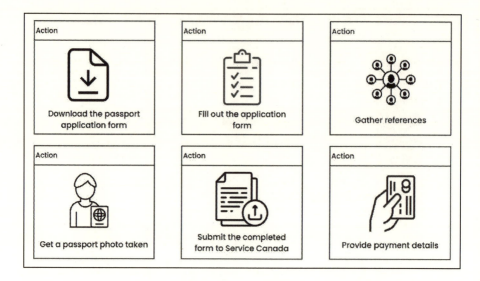

How your team storyboards is up to you and is largely determined by the number of iterations your team goes through in the prototyping phase.

Now let's look at wireframing. A wireframe is a skeletal image, or set of images, which displays the functional elements of a digital solution. Wireframes are used during the prototyping stage of the design thinking process to visually convey a digital solution.

The next example shows wireframes illustrating a popular ride-sharing app. Wireframes like these were likely used to create the initial prototypes for the ride-sharing apps you're familiar with today. The wireframes include all steps in the user journey, from ordering a ride to all the other screens within the app with which the user may interact.

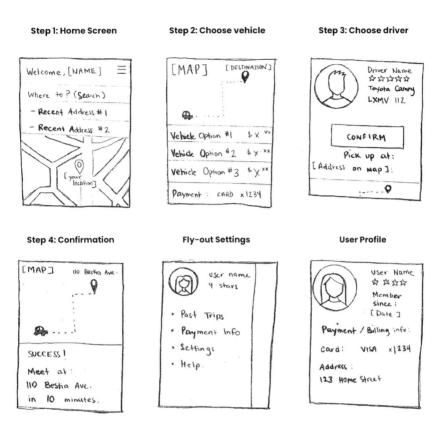

Here's another example of what a wireframe may have looked like during the creation of a government job bank mobile app. The wireframes visually represent the user journey from the app's home screen to the results screen, to further filtering the results and reviewing job details.

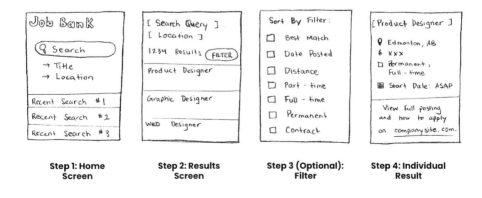

Entity Relationship Diagrams

An entity relationship diagram is a type of flow chart that illustrates how entities, such as people, objects, or concepts, relate to each other within a system. The entity relationship diagram can be used as a tool during the prototype phase of design thinking to sketch the design of a system or solution.

Entity relationship diagrams are different than the entity position maps, which are discussed in the ideate phase of this book. They sound similar but look different and are used in different parts of the design thinking process.

Here's an example of an entity relationship diagram of the passport application process, where the rectangles are entities (in this case, the applicant). Diamonds are actions taken by the entities. Ovals are attributes or data points associated with each action (applicants can download forms, complete forms, and submit forms). For a form to be completed it must contain the following data: Name, address, date of birth (DOB), references, and photo.

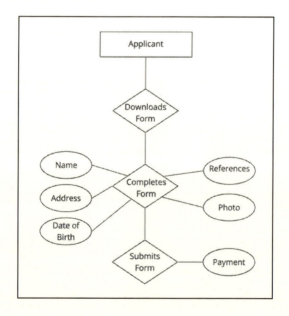

Design Thinking in Action: The Passport Application, Part 4

In the previous chapter, ideas were generated for our passport application scenario using rolestorming, a brainstorming technique. The next step is to create prototypes for the ideas we selected. The prototypes for our passport application process shown next are both low-fidelity types: Specifically, storyboard and wireframe.

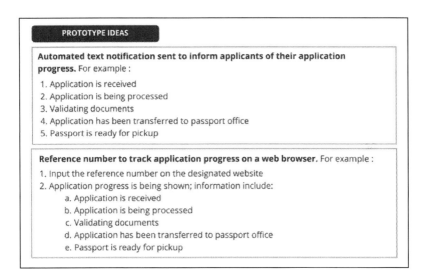

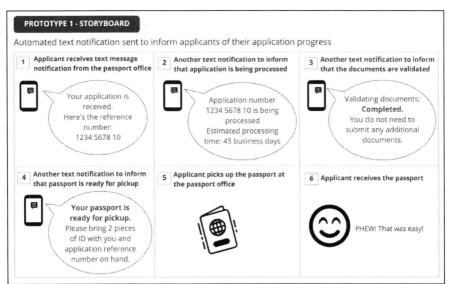

PROTOTYPE 2 - WIREFRAME

Reference number to track application progress on a web browser

Passport Application Tracking System

🔍 Search Reference Number

Search

Input reference number here

Help Support

📞 1-800-2020-72

✉ hello@passport.ca

💬 Chat with Live Agent

Passport Application Tracking System

Hello, Stevie

Your passport application status :

☑ Application is received — DD/MM/YYYY

☑ Documents are validated — DD/MM/YYYY

☑ Application is transferred to passport office — DD/MM/YYYY

☑ Passport is ready for pick up — DD/MM/YYYY

Pick up passport at **SERVICE CANADA**
885 Meadowlands Dr E unit 105, Ottawa, ON K2C 3N2

Book Appointment Here

Help Support

📞 1-800-2020-72

✉ hello@passport.ca

💬 Chat with Live Agent

Prototype Phase — Summary

In the fourth stage of the design thinking process, we discussed:

- Six types of prototypes
  - o Choosing the kind of prototype that best showcases an idea and its capabilities for end users

- Developing prototypes
  - o Building an idea into at least two prototypes to test and obtain feedback

- Storyboards and wireframing
  - o Visual representations of the steps and user experience of a solution prototype

- Entity relationship diagrams
  - o Illustrates the relationships between people, objects, or concepts within a system

The prototype phase takes us from abstract ideas to tangible solutions. Designers can bring their ideas to life by building prototypes that demonstrate specific aspects of the proposed solutions to their end users.

The developed prototypes are then tested by end users, which uncovers more about their needs and provides valuable insights into your approach while you continue to prototyping. Ideally more than one prototype is developed, giving users multiple options to test and compare.

Building and evaluating prototypes with end users will allow you to determine whether the prototyped solution effectively solves the originally defined problem, or if your team needs to revisit a previous phase to redefine or ideate before continuing the design process.

Step 5: Test

Testing Ideas with Users

Now that we've finished turning ideas into prototypes, we're ready to test them with end users! In this chapter we'll go over various types of testing, how to use testing for design thinking, and how to integrate feedback.

We've now covered all the phases of the design thinking process — from empathize, to define, ideate, and prototype.

It's now time to test, which is the final phase of the design thinking process.

Keep in mind that the purpose of testing prototypes is to get insights about end users and ensure prototypes solve their identified challenges. One additional thing to consider after the test phase is to determine if you need to revisit a previous phase of the design thinking process, or if you can proceed to implementation.

Let's determine the testing methods that will likely work best for your environment and prototypes, as well as how to test.

Companies in the private sector test their products all around us — often without us even realizing it.

Canada's Kingston, Ontario, for example, is a test market for consumer goods and services because of the wide range of university and college students from across the country in the city every year.

Testing can also be done with staff if you can't go to the general public.

James Dyson developed 5,126 prototypes for the cyclone that would form the basis of his revolutionary vacuum cleaner, with each version containing one small feature change at a time to see if it improved or reduced performance. He finally got it right, on the 5,127th attempt, after working methodically to find the best solution.

He was also testing to gauge whether the product worked, which is slightly different than design thinking prototyping and testing, but the same theory applies — start from one place and work methodically to find the best solutions.

In the public sector we want to find ways of making complex challenges as simple as possible by using design thinking to methodically work through them, while prototyping and testing along the way.

We've already mentioned the concept of low and high-fidelity prototypes (in our prototyping chapter). Prototypes become higher fidelity as they develop, and the same principle applies to testing. With each testing iteration we get more specific and granular about what we're testing for, and more micro around the types of questions being asked.

Your team may have heard of some of these tests before from engineering or science fields: Functional testing, quality assurance testing, assumption testing, testing biases, definition testing, and A/B testing. As an engineer, I've personally done a lot of these to see if something works and if it's doing what it is supposed to be doing.

Testing for Design Thinking

Design thinking testing is slightly different, however. It's about seeing how end users respond to prototypes. Before we get to design thinking testing, let's take a quick look at more traditional science and engineering testing methods.

When talking about testing most people mean functional testing — to see if something works. Design thinking testing, on the other hand, is meant to determine how end users perceive prototypes, how prototypes can be improved, and to gather new insights.

Examples of functional testing include wind tunnel testing to gauge the aerodynamics of vehicles or test building architecture against high winds. Functional testing can include testing communication technologies, such as a space agency testing how its communications systems might behave in space. Functional testing includes hardware testing — checking if components on a motherboard work, for example — or ruggedized testing, which involves testing for temperature and vibrational variations to make sure equipment can withstand different terrains and environments. This kind of testing is often employed for military hardware.

The types and levels of software testing, on the other hand, can range from testing super specific aspects to ensuring everything works well together. Software testing can include unit testing, function testing, integration testing, quality assurance testing, integration testing with other vendors, to quality assurance testing of the entire system.

In the public sector we work with services, policy, regulation, programs, processes, finance, IT, communication, documentation, stakeholder engagement, and much more. There are many things we need to prototype and test. During the testing phase we need to test not just functionality but also assumptions and biases, to ensure our prototype solves user challenges.

The private sector often performs assumption testing to identify assumptions around what people are willing to pay for something, or gauge product or service adoption rates. In the public sector it's not uncommon to test assumptions around the intended impact of a solution, and how much the solution may be adopted.

Assumption testing requires the collection of data, which includes identifying the data we need and figuring out how to get the data. Always be on guard against beliefs masquerading as facts, however — always test whether something is a belief or a fact in your assumption testing.

The testing phase is an opportunity to test team biases, as well. If your team develops empathy maps or journey maps for end clients before meeting them, and then compares what they learn to the maps they created, they may start to notice some unconscious biases. This is an opportunity to test and correct those biases.

In the public sector there are a lot of terms and definitions that could use enhancement. We can test these terms and definitions with end users during the testing phase! The intent is not to create the perfect definition, but to develop ideas on what else needs to be included and what can be excluded.

Putting rudimentary definitions in front of participants, so they can identify ways of making the definition better, can help speed up the process while also testing definitions.

A/B testing is a type of testing many of us know well. It involves having two versions (A and B) of something and comparing them to one another. They're generally identical except for one variation that might affect a user's behaviour. Version A might be the currently used version (control), while version B is modified in some respect (treatment).

We might see A/B testing on an e-commerce website where businesses want to improve the buying experience for customers.

Small things are tested one at a time, such as content, layouts, images, and colours. Companies such as Uber, Netflix, and Airbnb perform A/B testing live and continuously without most people noticing.

In the public sector the same methodology is applied. For example, with a cross-government web renewal project we worked on, multiple versions of web page elements were developed and tested with end clients. Variables around search and display methods were part of this A/B testing.

The power of A/B testing can be illustrated through something as simple as changing the order of contact information, which can have a significant impact on the operational cost of an organization. One local business reduced its support cost by $10,000 a month by switching the order of its contact information on its website. Instead of displaying phone number first, the company provided an email address for people to submit an online help request.

As your team tests with end clients, ensure they know you aren't committed to building any of the prototypes being tested. Make sure they know this is more about getting their feedback to either create different solutions or improve what's already in place. This gives your team the flexibility to change as you get more insights.

Coming up with a set of questions beforehand is one of the best practices to obtain constructive evaluation from users. Here are some examples of questions to ask:

- Does the prototype address your needs?
- Would you like to be communicated to by text, or through our website?
- Which prototype do you like best and why?
- What do you like about each prototype and why?
- What would you change to improve each of the prototypes?

- Is there something that would make each of the prototypes even better?

Depending on the result of the test and feedback from the users, we can then decide whether to take a step back to review the previous design thinking phases, do reiterations of prototyping and testing, or implement the prototypes with improvements.

Remember, a prototype doesn't need to be high-fidelity at the beginning. Simple drawings can provide a plethora of insights and information.

Also consider testing by persona. Understanding each persona's reactions to a prototype can be valuable. Try to get as close to the persona's typical environment as possible during the test. For example, if the persona normally uses the service in a loud, busy, noisy area, make sure your team tests the solution in a similar environment for that persona. If your team can't get personas to be involved, then try testing internally within your organization.

We know a software company that used its iOS developers to test Android versions of its app, and Android developers to test the iOS version. The developers found inconsistencies in the two processes and aesthetics, including where buttons were placed on the screen. These new insights allowed them to improve their product. Always consider opportunities to test processes and services internally within your own organization.

As your team tests, also consider how to gather feedback. Will your team test in person or remotely? What questions will your team ask in terms of how they interact with prototypes? How will your team record the feedback? Try to get end users that developed your empathy maps and personas to also be testers, so it comes full circle.

For example, if your team selected a web page to do A and B wireframe prototypes, then test with the end users or with another team.

They can use software to track where end users' eyes go on the wireframe or have someone ask questions on testers' impressions of the wireframes. If your team uses software, it will automatically record the information for them. If your team observes and asks questions, they'll need assistance to capture the tester's responses.

Remember to monitor and evaluate as you're testing. Ask users what they observed and ask probing questions as they use the prototypes. Identify what your team observes as end users complete their tests. Is there one prototype that works better than others? Why? Ask testers, and your team, what was learned during testing.

Make sure to track your test results, write down observations along the way, have a list of questions to ask, and feel free to go off-script to discover reasoning behind a tester's decisions, thoughts, and thought process. Remember: It's about getting insights to make products, services, and policies even better.

Examples Of Testing in The Public Sector

Labeling and Reporting of Energy Efficiency In Homes

Natural Resources Canada (NRCan)'s Social Innovation UnLab partnered with the Province of Alberta's CoLab and the City of Edmonton to improve the labeling and reporting of energy efficiency in homes. They co-designed and tested prototypes with citizens, with efforts centred around redesigning the federal EnerGuide based on user-identified issues.

In the first project, user research indicated a need to re-evaluate the effectiveness of EnerGuide labels in communicating information. Homeowners in three Canadian provinces were shown one of three labels: Canada's EnerGuide, the U.S. Home Energy Score, and the U.K.'s Energy Performance Certification.

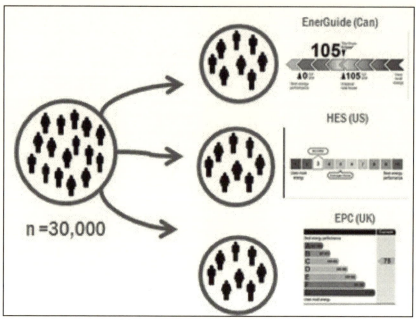

Source: https://exp-works.medium.com/our-ew-experience-is-ending-our-experimentation-journey-continues-716a10e7a420

Reading comprehension was measured on whether the respondents could correctly answer questions about the information on the labels. For example, to the question "Is the house represented by this label energy efficient?" only 62 percent of EnerGuide users could correctly answer, compared to 82 percent with the U.S. label and 74 percent with the U.K. label. Researchers noted that while the EnerGuide label offers more information, it's also less clear in its energy rating scale. The knowledge gained from this testing showed that users often have trouble interpreting the EnerGuide label, suggesting the need for further iteration and improvement.

In the second project, homeowners in the same three provinces were tested to see if message framing impacted the number of users that sought a home energy evaluation service. Their variation of A/B testing included three options: A control group, a cost-framed group, and a comfort-framed group.

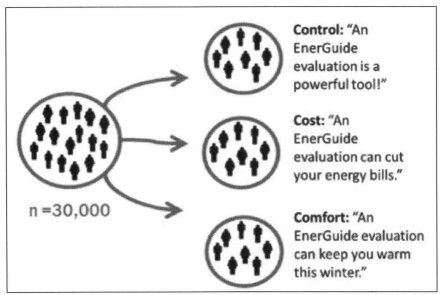

Source: https://exp-works.medium.com/our-ew-experience-is-ending-our-experimentation-journey-continues-716a10e7a420

The control group click-through rate was 77.8 percent, while the cost-framed messaging was 78.9 percent, and the comfort-framed messaging rate was 78.7 percent. The conclusion was that no distinct differences were made by message framing.

Finland's Basic Income Experiments

During a basic income experiment conducted in Finland, 2,000 unemployed people were paid a tax-exempt income of 560 Euros (about $830 CAD) monthly, regardless of any other income or whether they were actively looking for work.

The experiment — which essentially was one big test — was implemented by Kela, Finland's social insurance institution, to examine the outcome of a universal basic income to replace unemployment benefits. "The aim was to study how it would be possible to reshape the Finnish social security system so that it better meets the challenges posed by changes in working life," Kela wrote in its report on the experiment.

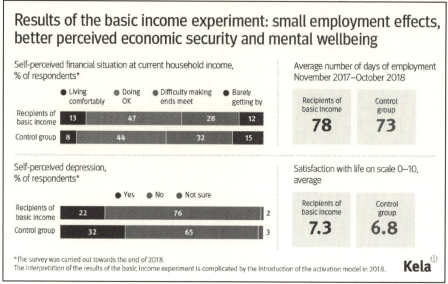

Source: https://www.weforum.org/agenda/2020/05/finlands-basic-income-trial-
found-people-were-happier-but-werent-more-likely-to-get-jobs/

After considering many factors, Kela concluded that the effect of a universal basic income on employment was small.

Basic income receivers were more satisfied with life; went through less depression, sadness, and loneliness; and had a more positive perception of their ability to concentrate, memorize and learn. The testing was successful in that it provided new information and insight, as well as proof that large-scale social experiments can be done from a legislative perspective.

Singapore's Employment Pass

Applying for an Employment Pass in Singapore used to be a tedious, 13-step procedure full of long waits and confusing paperwork. In 2009, however, the process underwent a drastic redesign that incorporated design thinking principles[7]. The country remodelled its application as an experience by looking at applicants as people with lives, needs, and feelings — not as units to be moved from one step to the next.

After gathering field observations of the existing system, various solutions were prototyped and tested with applicants, staff, and employers. One insight gained was that applicants value information and certainty. From this, two adjustments were made: The online portal was reworked to increase information flow to users, and visits to the employment center in Singapore became appointment-based.

Employing a user-centric approach for redesigning Singapore's Employment Pass application process went beyond decreased waiting times and improved applicant experiences. The government also transformed the public's perception of it being a high-handed employment regulator, instead portraying itself as a transparent and responsive employment facilitator that cares for its applicants.

Stanford's Winnebago Experiment

The Golden Gate Regional Center (GGRC) provides support to people with developmental disabilities in the San Francisco area. For the parents of children with disabilities, obtaining GGRC services previously required at least three months of meetings, assessments, examinations — often distressing the children and causing their parents to abandon the venture.[8]

Recognizing a need for improvement, two students from Stanford's Hasso Plattner Institute of Design (also known as d.school) worked with the team to streamline the assessment process. The highlight of the project was the Winnebago experiment, which involved two students and eight staff piling into a Winnebago to visit potential clients and assess their eligibility for services.

With everyone together in the Winnebago families could meet with each staff member at the same time, dramatically enhancing client experiences. This also allowed the staff to better support each other's work. It provided the opportunity for each case to be discussed from different perspectives, leading to faster and better decision-making. The team completed nine assessments in two hours and the previous three-month process was reduced to 10 weeks.

From Failure to Insight

Winston Churchill once said that "success consists of going from failure to failure without loss of enthusiasm," and he was right. Keep prototyping and testing. It's okay to have multiple iterations, especially as you go from low fidelity to high fidelity. While it can sometimes be discouraging to take so much time up front, it will save you a lot more time and money (and heartache) later.

But what if all your prototypes fail?

Asking end users why a prototype doesn't solve their challenge brings forward new insights and additional information. It's also an indicator that your team needs to go back in the design thinking process and re-iterate. Where in the process to go back to depends on the type of feedback you receive.

Also make sure to integrate the feedback. What has your team learned from end clients? What does the information clients provided indicate or signal? Is there a clear winner? Are there things your team should incorporate or explore?

Design Thinking in Action: The Passport Application, Part 5

Back to our passport application once again! We've now gone from the empathizing phase after creating a persona, an unarticulated needs map/empathy map, and a journey map of Stevie's passport renewal application, to defining Stevie's pain points and reframing the challenge from the organization's point of view using the HMW technique.

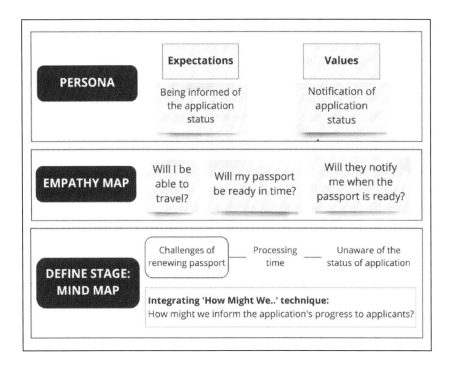

We then generated solutions through a spinoff of the rolestorming technique, by using an IT industry leader to come up with several ideas to address the problem. Two prototypes were then presented to illustrate these solutions in the form of a storyboard and wireframe.

The next step is testing the prototypes to gain feedback and substantiate whether the prototypes solve the users' needs. Showcase the test notification (storyboard) and tracking application (wireframe) prototypes to end users.

Questions to ask could include:

- Do you think these prototypes would provide you enough information to feel informed about your application's status?
- Which of the two prototypes do you prefer? Why?
- Is there anything else you would like to see in these prototypes?

Listen to their responses and insights to determine if one of the prototypes will be implemented, or if one or both prototypes need to be revised.

The passport application example has demonstrated how design thinking can help address Stevie's challenges. This creative problem-solving methodology highlights the importance of user-centred design by emphasizing the need to understand the users and their journey, and allowing for co-creation that benefits both parties to further improve the product, service, or policy.

Summary — Test Phase

In the fifth and final stage of the design thinking process we have discussed:

Types of testing
- Determining what methods work best for your environment and prototypes

How to test
- Testing assumptions, biases, and ensuring that the prototype solves real challenges for end users

Integrating feedback
- Learning from your end users on how to improve, and iterating as needed

The testing phase is when your team can test a solution's impact with end users. The feedback and insights provided are essential to understanding how end users perceive and use the prototype. As you observe your users' responses, your team can learn what changes are needed to improve the solution before implementation.

It is very likely that additional issues and needs will be uncovered during the testing phase. Design thinking allows the re-iteration of previous phases to redevelop prototypes and continue testing until the desired outcome is achieved. This should result in successful delivery of the best solution to your end users: In other words, happy clients!

Better Services Through Service Design

We've now gone through the entire design thinking process: We've empathized with users, created journey maps, and defined the challenge to solve. Through ideation, prototyping, and testing, we've also determined the service we want to create.

We now know we need to implement a service — or re-design an existing service and how — to meet users' needs. With that in mind, let's look at the basics of service design, how it relates to the design thinking process, and how to use it to your advantage. We'll also examine service blueprints and how they can help when designing services that delight users.

Like design thinking, service design is a design methodology. But while design thinking and service design are often used interchangeably, there are some key differences. For one thing, design thinking is a high-level methodology used when facing a challenge where you're unsure what to do, or when the way forward is unclear. The design thinking process is unrestricted by the parameters of a pre-determined solution. If we know we need to create a service as an outcome, we'll apply design thinking principles as we design or enhance that service.

Service design, on the other hand, is about the planning and organizing of people, infrastructure, communication, and material elements of a service to improve its quality and the interaction between the service provider and users. Service design is typically implemented after using design thinking to determine what the service will look like. Design thinking is the overarching methodology of discovering key aspects within the problem space, before delving deeper through service design.

Creating Service Blueprints

A number of public-sector organizations facilitate direct services to the public such as passports, tax centres, veterans benefits, and licensing. Several public sector organizations also have services directed internally.

With that in mind, let's look at service blueprints — which, if your team already has an existing service, are based on an existing user journey map. In service design, user journey maps are used to visually display a user's service experience, including all interactions and touchpoints of both the users and employees.

Service design blueprints are useful for visualizing complex or multichannel service offerings to better understand the issues and areas in need of improvement during the user journey. Blueprints delve deeper into the user journey to identify all processes, both visible and invisible to the user, that occur and how they relate to each other.

Why create service blueprints? They can help redesign an old, outdated service. They're also extremely useful for providing clarity on who does what, where, and when, from the start of the service to the end. They provide insight on where issues typically occur, as well as showcase both high-level and minute details of a process to increase flexibility and scalability. This level of detail helps illustrate the bigger picture, especially within large organizations with complex processes or services.

Service design looks at the user journey by using an existing journey map, while also accounting for the range of employee roles and internal processes within an organization. Service design covers both physical and digital environments. For example, in a passport renewal service, the service encompasses both the website where the user downloads the application forms and the passport office itself.

Service design seeks to optimize usability and sustainability for both employees and users in all delivery channels. In our passport application example, this means creating an optimal user experience for applicants navigating the passport service website, for applicants at the passport office, and for employees who work on passport applications.

Let's look at this fictitious service blueprint for Starbucks (we'll look at a public sector application in our use case at the end of the chapter). For this section we've taken liberties to interpret what the Starbucks service blueprint could look like — but keep in mind that service blueprints can differ even from coffee shop to coffee shop!

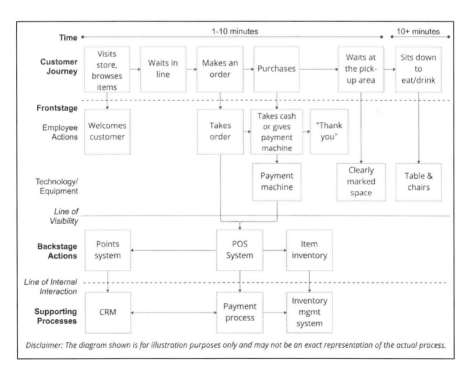

The service blueprint starts when the customer enters the store, at which point the employee welcomes them. The customer waits in line and then purchases, during which the employee takes the order and inputs information into the point of sale (POS) system. The POS system is a backstage action taken by the employee, as this is something the customer cannot see — hence the line of visibility in the diagram.

The information entered in the POS system affects the computer's inventory system and tracks the customer's reward points. Again, these aspects are invisible to the customer but vital to the service experience.

Supporting processes include entities related to any systems used. For example, the points system is likely managed by a customer relationship management (CRM) system. The item inventory is probably connected to an inventory management system, which can be configured to automatically order items running low at that store.

Upon completing payment, the customer waits in the pick-up area and then sits down to eat or drink. We see the employee plays an important frontstage role by keeping the store clean for the customer at all times.

Let's look at all the individual parts of a service blueprint, starting with our user's actions. The highlighted horizontal sections below are referred to as swim lanes. The user journey swim lane lists all the actions the user takes during the service experience, including all touchpoints in chronological order. If timing is integral to your service, then include a timeline in the blueprint, as well.

The lines in a service blueprint not only separate each swim lane, but also denote points of interaction and visibility. Using our coffee shop example, we see that when the customer makes a purchase, they can interact with the employee and payment machine. This interaction is separated by the dashed line.

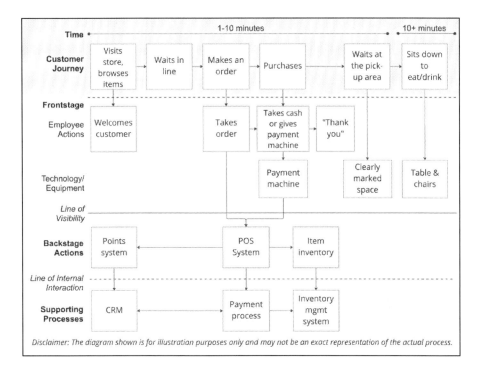

Disclaimer: The diagram shown is for illustration purposes only and may not be an exact representation of the actual process.

The solid line of visibility demonstrates which aspects of the service are out of sight but still activated. Think of the sections below the line of visibility as the crew behind the curtain of a theatre show: The customer cannot see the POS and inventory systems, but they support the user journey in the background, much like how stagehands move props between scenes.

The line of internal interaction between backstage actions and supporting processes illustrates where supporting processes (or employees who do not encounter the user) support the journey. In our example, this refers to the connection between the points system activated by the user's purchase and the CRM, which is a separate supporting process. The arrows show the relationship and dependencies between each element.

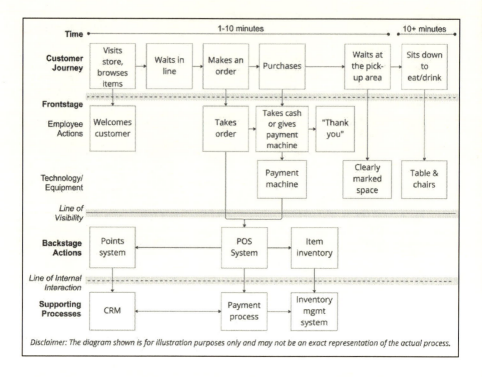

Disclaimer: The diagram shown is for illustration purposes only and may not be an exact representation of the actual process.

The frontstage actions are those taken by the employee, as well as technology or equipment, that the customer can see. In our coffee example, the customer can interact with both the employee and the debit machine.

The backstage actions are those which the customer cannot see — for example, the employee inputting the customer's order into the POS system.

The supporting processes swim lane shows the organizational processes that support the employee providing service to user. The customer's purchase earns them points, which is tied to a separate system — the organization's CRM. Same goes for the POS system linked to the store's inventory management system, which automatically re-orders items when they're running low.

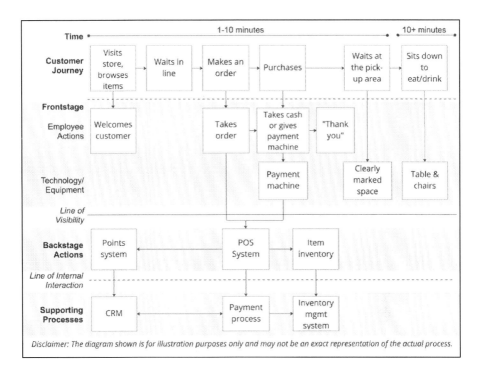

Disclaimer: The diagram shown is for illustration purposes only and may not be an exact representation of the actual process.

What are some things to consider as you build a service blueprint? If your team is documenting a current service, use current journey maps as reference material. If your team is designing a new one, reference your future or ideal journey maps.

As in the case of creating personas or empathy maps, we also recommend co-creating service blueprints with users. Research alongside your stakeholders by including users and employees involved in the journey to ensure accurate representation of all elements within the blueprint. Share these blueprints with decision-makers. Blueprints are helpful for clarifying exactly what takes place, and when, during the service or process.

Jump into service blueprinting to map out the process step-by-step if you already know the solution is a service and how that service should look after completing your future journey maps, prototypes and tests.

If you're unsure what your solution should look like, or where to start, use the design thinking process to explore the challenge further. This will allow you to find a tailored solution unique to your organization. Design thinking can also help develop a shared language as you go through the process and arrive at a common goal.

Remember, use a current journey map if you'd like to document an existing service, or a future journey map that's been prototyped and tested if you'd like to create or re-design a service.

Current journey maps support an understanding a client's current journey (as-is state), while future journey maps may be useful for showing how the selected solution will improve the journey (to-be state). A future journey map is all you need if you're creating a totally new service.

Design Thinking in Action: The Passport Application, Part 6

Let's look at the service blueprint for our passport renewal application process. We've highlighted the customer journey maps in the previous chapter, and the next step is to visualize the human and technology touchpoints, supporting services, and physical and digital processes behind Stevie's customer journey.

In the diagram, we illustrate a 'to-be' service blueprint of implementing one of the prototype solutions we came up with earlier. The proposed solution is informing the applicant of the status of their passport application through text messages. This method shows the broad picture of how a service is provided by an organization (at all levels) and utilized by users.

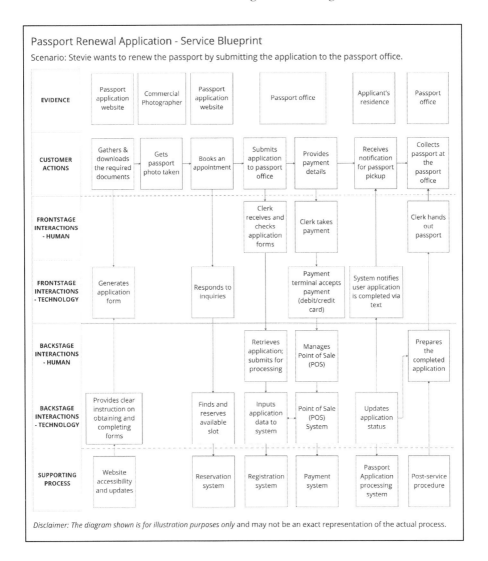

Passport Renewal Application - Service Blueprint

Scenario: Stevie wants to renew the passport by submitting the application to the passport office.

EVIDENCE	Passport application website	Commercial Photographer	Passport application website	Passport office		Applicant's residence	Passport office
CUSTOMER ACTIONS	Gathers & downloads the required documents	Gets passport photo taken	Books an appointment	Submits application to passport office	Provides payment details	Receives notification for passport pickup	Collects passport at the passport office
FRONTSTAGE INTERACTIONS - HUMAN				Clerk receives and checks application forms	Clerk takes payment		Clerk hands out passport
FRONTSTAGE INTERACTIONS - TECHNOLOGY	Generates application form		Responds to inquiries		Payment terminal accepts payment (debit/credit card)	System notifies user application is completed via text	
BACKSTAGE INTERACTIONS - HUMAN				Retrieves application; submits for processing	Manages Point of Sale (POS)		Prepares the completed application
BACKSTAGE INTERACTIONS - TECHNOLOGY	Provides clear instruction on obtaining and completing forms		Finds and reserves available slot	Inputs application data to system	Point of Sale (POS) System	Updates application status	
SUPPORTING PROCESS	Website accessibility and updates		Reservation system	Registration system	Payment system	Passport Application processing system	Post-service procedure

Disclaimer: The diagram shown is for illustration purposes only and may not be an exact representation of the actual process.

Summary — Better Services (Service Design)

In this section, we have discussed:

- What service design is
    - Examining the complete service journey to optimize the experience for both the user and employees

- How service design relates to design thinking
    - Using both methodologies to create services that meet users' needs

- Service design blueprints
    - Mapping the interactions and processes within a user's service experience

Once you've used the design thinking process to determine what the service looks like, you can implement service design to further refine the service. By planning and organizing all the elements of a service the quality of interactions between the service provider and users can be improved.

Service design blueprints are important tools that identify all interactions, touchpoints, and technology systems that users and employees engage with. Visualizing the relationships between complex or multi-channel service offerings allow you to better understand problem areas and the adaptations needed to improve the user journey.

As in design thinking, co-creation is one of the foundations of successful service design. Remember to invite people who will use and interact with your service. Obtaining user input will enhance the overall innovation and service experience.

Conclusion

Citizens and those in the public sector using other departments' services, processes, and policies have different needs, expectations, and measures of success. To improve their experiences, a design thinking mindset and methodology is essential.

As leaders, understanding mindset and methodology is key for making programs more successful and creating a winning culture for teams and organizations. Design thinking can help with this. Indeed, design thinking is a human-centred design tool that looks at end users' perspectives before defining what the service, process, project, or policy looks like.

When people are asked how to improve a service they often ask for something more user-friendly. What that means, however, varies for each person and each service — whether we're talking about easier access, easier understanding, or easier navigation. Asking deeper questions and listening to end users helps define better service. This is vital for creating effective, efficient services — even more so as different departments and levels of government continue to integrate services, processes, and policies. This also has a massive impact on reducing barriers, information silos, and regulatory burdens.

Public-sector and government environments are complex and constantly changing, so it can be difficult to know where to start.

The design thinking roadmap helps you get your bearings by looking at end users first — whether they're citizens, businesses, other government departments or other levels of government — to blaze a path toward understanding what needs to be done to create better experiences.

Begin your understanding of users by identifying them, developing personas, and creating empathy maps of each user type to determine their articulated and unarticulated needs. The journeys of each end user type will likely be different. Capturing these journeys helps identify all issues, along with which challenges impact multiple types of end clients. This is the foundation for articulating opportunities to explore. Spending time understanding the challenge through understanding end users allows us to better articulate what needs to be solved in a clear, concise, and better scoped-out manner. This process ensures we solve the right issues from the start — rather than creating solutions for the wrong challenges or solving symptoms rather than root causes.

Once an issue is articulated it becomes much easier to devise a solution, prototype it, and test that solution. Prototyping and testing provide many insights into end users and whether your solution will work. These prototypes and tests don't need to be intricate.

Capturing observations and insights supports the creation of even better services, processes, and policies in the future. Incorporating different perspectives, especially the human perspective, and reframing challenges provides new insights and opportunities for moving forward, updating, modernizing, and future-proofing the public sector.

Finally, always remember that design thinking is iterative — and that nothing stays the same. We want to continue understanding our end users as they and their environments continually change, meaning your services, processes, and policies must change with them as new information is learned.

Bibliography

Brown, B. (2018). *Dare to Lead: Brave Work. Tough Conversations. Whole Hearts.* Random House.

Gerlsbeck, R. (2019). *A Little Nudge Goes a Long Way.* Retrieved from Smith Magazine: https://smith.queensu.ca/magazine/issues/winter-2019/features/playing-win.php

Goleman, D., McKee, A., Waytz, A., & Harvard Business Review. (2017). *Empathy (HBR Emotional Intelligence Series).* Harvard Business Review Press .

Gwee, J. (2010, August 14). *Redesigning the Service Experience.* Retrieved from Civil Service College Singapore: https://www.csc.gov.sg/articles/redesigning-the-service-experience

KELA. (2020, May 6). Retrieved from Results of Finland's Basic Income Experiment: Small Employment Effect, Better Perceived Economic Security and Mental Wellbeing: https://www.kela.fi/web/en/news-archive/-/asset_publisher/lN08GY2nIrZo/content/results-of-the-basicincome-experiment-small-employment-effects-better-perceived-economic-security-and-mental-wellbeing.

Liedtka, J. (2013). *Solving Problems with Design Thinking: Ten Stories of What Works.* Columbia Business School Publishing.

NRCan Team. (2019, May 16). *Experimentation Works.* Retrieved from Our EW Experience is Ending, Our Experimentation Journey Continues: https://exp-works.medium.com/our-ew-experience-is-ending-our-experimentation-journey-continues-716a10e7a420

Sutton, R., & Hoyt, D. (2016, January 6). Retrieved from Harvard Business Review : https://hbr.org/2016/01/better-service-faster-a-design-thinking-case-study

Zeballos-Roig, J. (2020, May 8). Retrieved from World Economic Forum: https://www.weforum.org/agenda/2020/05/finlands-basic-income-trial-found-people-were-happier-but-werent-more-likely-to-get-jobs/

Endnotes

1. Brené Brown, *Dare to Lead: Brave Words. Tough Conversations. Whole Hearts* (New York: Random House Publishing Group, 2018), 4.

2. Daniel Goleman, *What is Empathy (HBR Emotional Intelligence Series)* (Boston: Harvard Business Review Press, 2017), 1-3.

3. A.G. Lafley and Roger Martin, *Playing to Win: How Strategy Really Works* (Harvard Business Review Press, 2013), 136

4. Emma Seppala, *Why Compassion Is a Better Managerial Tactic Than Toughness (HBR Emotional Intelligence Series)* (Boston: Harvard Business Review Press, 2017), 20

5. Brené Brown, *Integration Idea-Empathy* (Brené Brown LLC, 2020), 2 document retrieved from https://brenebrown.com/resources/empathy

6. Rob Gerlsbeck, *A Little Nudge Goes a Long Way* (Kingston: The Stephen J.R. Smith School of Business, 2019),14

7. June Gwee, *Redesigning the Service Experience* (Singapore: Civil Service College, 2010), page 66-72

8. Robert I. Sutton and David Hoyt, *Better Service, Faster: A Design Thinking Case Study* (Harvard Business Review, 2016) article retrieved from hbr.org/2016/01/better-service-faster-a-design-thinking-case-study

Acknowledgements

I am very thankful for all the people that have helped in creating this book and that have supported my journey in building and growing Spring2 Innovation.

I am grateful for all the support of my team, our partners, mentors, coaches, and our fantastic clients who have trusted us with their initiatives.

There are a few people that were instrumental in creating this book that I want to thank specifically: Osa Insani, David Booker, Donna Wood, Jessica Madden, Jessica Schultz, Jessica Perreault, Kim Ennis, Liz McKeown, Jason Mombourquette, Todd Hunter, Mark Sutcliffe and Michelle Smart. I'd also like to thank my editor, Jim Donnelly, for his work on this book. And my support and test team at home — Ethan and Aydin.

A special thanks to David Perry for supporting and encouraging me over the years to write and publish a book about design thinking.

There are a lot more people who had a part and input in my journey. You know who you are. Thank you!

I am most gratified that our work is changing people's perspectives and how they perceive the world. People feel more empowered and capable of overcoming obstacles after participating in our training or working on projects with us.

Thank you all for your dedication, hard work, insights, support and energy. I appreciate all of you more than you can imagine.

Resources

Design Thinking Tools & Templates

Available at futureproofingbydesign.com

Design Thinking Training Programs

Introduction to Design Thinking (Online):
https://spring2innovation.com/public-sector/public-sector-courses/introduction-to-design-thinking

Design Thinking for the Public Sector (Level 1):
https://spring2innovation.com/public-sector/public-sector-courses/design-thinking-for-the-public-sector-level-1

Design Thinking Certification:
https://spring2innovation.com/public-sector/public-sector-courses/public-sector-design-thinking-certification

Design Thinking YouTube Videos

Design Thinking for Complex Environments | Nilufer Erdebil TEDxOttawa
Steps of Design Thinking | Spring2 Innovation
A Look Inside A Design Thinker's Toolkit | Spring2 Innovation

Additional design thinking programs and resources available at
www.spring2innovation.com

About the Author

Nilufer Erdebil is the founder and CEO of Spring2 Innovation, a training and consulting firm specializing in design thinking. She is also an award-winning design thinking expert and a TEDx and TEC/Vistage speaker. For over twenty-five years she has been a catalyst for innovation. She has worked extensively with public and private sector organizations to drive strategy, facilitate change and introduce new products and services. Her experience working within different fields including telecommunications, application development, program management and IT management give her a deep understanding of the business challenges today's organizations are faced with.

Nilufer has successfully developed and facilitated design thinking sessions that address human-centric challenges. Her expertise provides clarity for organizations to define the true challenge and generate innovative solutions. From employee engagement, starting new initiatives, policy development to digital transformation, she is passionate about driving cultural change and creating user-centred strategies for organizations to overcome roadblocks and achieve optimum results.

Nilufer is a 2014 recipient of the Ottawa Business Journal Forty Under 40 Award and a 2016 recipient of the WCT Leadership Award from Women in Communications and Technology. She is a Professional Engineer with a Bachelor of Science in Electrical Engineering and an MBA from Queen's University.

Nilufer is most proud of her two kids Ethan and Aydin.

Manufactured by Amazon.ca
Bolton, ON